THE SHOOTING SCRIPT®

# GOSFORD PARK

Director Robert Altman and screenwriter Julian Fellowes on the set of *Gosford Park*

# GOSFORD PARK

SCREENPLAY AND AFTERWORD BY
JULIAN FELLOWES

INTRODUCTION BY
ROBERT ALTMAN

A Newmarket Shooting Script® Series Book
NEWMARKET PRESS • NEW YORK

Screenplay based upon an idea by Robert Altman and Bob Balaban.
All stills photographs by Mark Tillie.



This book is published simultaneously in the United States of America and in Canada.



FIRST EDITION

02 03 04 10 9 8 7 6 5 4 3 2

ISBN: 1-55704-531-3 (paperback)

02 03 04 10 9 8 7 6 5 4 3 2 1

ISBN: 1-55704-547-X (hardcover)

Library of Congress Catalog-in-Publication Data is available upon request.

QUANTITY PURCHASES

Companies, professional groups, clubs, and other organizations may qualify for special terms when ordering quantities of this title. For information, write to Special Sales, Newmarket Press, 18 East 48th Street, New York, NY 10017; call (212) 832-3575 or 1-800-669-3903; FAX (212) 832-3629; or e-mail mailbox@newmarketpress.com.
Website: www.newmarketpress.com

Manufactured in the United States of America.

OTHER BOOKS IN THE NEWMARKET SHOOTING SCRIPT® SERIES INCLUDE:

*The Age of Innocence: The Shooting Script*
*American Beauty: The Shooting Script*
*A Beautiful Mind: The Shooting Script*
*The Birdcage: The Shooting Script*
*Black Hawk Down: The Shooting Script*
*Cast Away: The Shooting Script*
*Dead Man Walking: The Shooting Script*
*Erin Brockovich: The Shooting Script*
*Gods and Monsters: The Shooting Script*
*Human Nature: The Shooting Script*
*The Ice Storm: The Shooting Script*
*Knight's Tale: The Shooting Script*
*Man on the Moon: The Shooting Script*
*The Matrix: The Shooting Script*
*Nurse Betty: The Shooting Script*
*The People vs. Larry Flynt: The Shooting Script*
*The Shawshank Redemption: The Shooting Script*
*Snatch: The Shooting Script*
*Snow Falling on Cedars: The Shooting Script*
*State and Main: The Shooting Script*
*Traffic: The Shooting Script*
*The Truman Show: The Shooting Script*

OTHER NEWMARKET PICTORIAL MOVIEBOOKS AND NEWMARKET INSIDER FILM BOOKS INCLUDE:

*The Age of Innocence: A Portrait of the Film**
*ALI: The Movie and The Man**
*Amistad: A Celebration of the Film by Steven Spielberg*
*The Art of The Matrix**
*Bram Stoker's Dracula: The Film and the Legend**
*Cradle Will Rock: The Movie and the Moment**
*Crouching Tiger, Hidden Dragon: A Portrait of the Ang Lee Film**
*Dances with Wolves: The Illustrated Story of the Epic Film**
*E.T. The Extra-Terrestrial from Concept to Classic: The Illustrated Story of the Film and Filmmakers**
*Gladiator: The Making of the Ridley Scott Epic Film*
*The Jaws Log*
*Men in Black: The Script and the Story Behind the Film**
*Neil Simon's Lost in Yonkers: The Illustrated Screenplay of the Film**
*Planet of The Apes: Re-imagined by Tim Burton**
*Saving Private Ryan: The Men, The Mission, The Movie*
*The Sense and Sensibility Screenplay & Diaries**
*The Seven Years in Tibet Screenplay and Story**
*Stuart Little: The Art, the Artists and the Story Behind the Amazing Movie**
*Windtalkers: The Making of the Film about the Navajo Code Talkers of World War II*

**Includes Screenplay*

CONTENTS

## BY ROBERT ALTMAN

In the fall of 1999, Bob Balaban and I had the idea of making an Agatha Christie-style murder mystery told from the point of view of the servants in the house. It's impossible to imagine a writer who could have brought more authority and talent to this premise than Julian Fellowes.

With his script for *Gosford Park*, Julian furnished the country home for all of us—a great imaginative accommodation that the actors, the designers, and I could move into, ramble around, live in, and make our own.

Julian did us the extra service of being on set almost every day of the shoot, helping us to understand the manners of the day (about which he is enormously knowledgeable), and rewriting and revising as we went—to trace and reinvent important aspects of the story that otherwise might have been lost as the film changed and evolved.

Julian's singular knowledge of the period, the wonderful characters he put on the page (which our terrific cast brought so beautifully to life), and the diction of these people, which Julian entirely owns, helped create the bedrock for a film that has truly been one of the great experiences of my life.

# ABOVE STAIRS

Michael Gambon
SIR WILLIAM McCORDLE
Owner of Gosford Park
Husband of Sylvia

## FAMILY

Maggie Smith
CONSTANCE
The Countess of Trentham
Aunt of the Three Sisters:
Sylvia, Louisa & Lavinia

Kristin Scott Thomas
LADY SYLVIA McCORDLE
Wife of Sir William McCordle
Mother of Isobel
One of the Three Sisters

Geraldine Somerville
LOUISA, LADY STOCKBRIDGE
Wife of Lord Stockbridge
One of the Three Sisters

Natasha Wightman
LADY LAVINIA MEREDITH
Wife of Lt. Commander Anthony Meredith
One of the Three Sisters

Camilla Rutherford
ISOBEL McCORDLE
Daughter of Sir William & Lady Sylvia

Charles Dance
RAYMOND, LORD STOCKBRIDGE
Husband of Louisa

Tom Hollander
LT. COMMANDER ANTHONY MEREDITH
Husband of Lavinia

Stephen Fry
INSPECTOR THOMPSON
The Police Inspector

## GUESTS

Bob Balaban
MORRIS WEISSMAN
Hollywood Movie Producer

Jeremy Northam
IVOR NOVELLO
Cousin of Sir William McCordle
Popular Composer & Matinee Idol

James Wilby
HON. FREDDIE NESBITT
Husband of Mabel

Claudie Blakley
MABEL NESBITT
Wife of Hon. Freddie Nesbitt

Laurence Fox
LORD RUPERT STANDISH
Suitor to Isobel McCordle

Trent Ford
JEREMY BLOND
Cunning Friend of Lord Rupert Standish

# BELOW STAIRS

## GOSFORD PARK SERVANTS

Alan Bates
JENNINGS
The Butler

Helen Mirren
MRS. WILSON
The Housekeeper

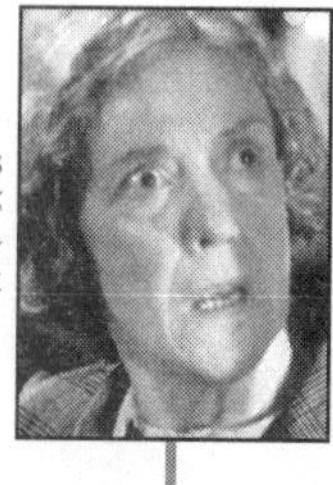

Eileen Atkins
MRS. CROFT
The Cook

Richard E. Grant
GEORGE
First Footman

Jeremy Swift
ARTHUR
Second Footman

Derek Jacobi
PROBERT
Sir William McCordle's Valet

Emily Watson
ELSIE
Head Housemaid

Meg Wynn Owen
LEWIS
Lady Sylvia McCordle's Maid

Sophie Thompson
DOROTHY
The Still Room Maid

Teresa Churcher
BERTHA
Head Kitchen Maid

Ron Webster
CONSTABLE DEXTER
The Junior Officer

## VISITING SERVANTS

Kelly Macdonald
MARY MACEACHRAN
Constance's Maid

Clive Owen
ROBERT PARKS
Lord Stockbridge's Valet

Adrian Scarborough
BARNES
Lt. Commander Meredith's Valet

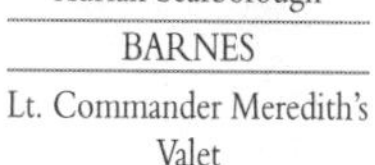

Ryan Phillippe
HENRY DENTON
Morris Weissman's Valet

# GOSFORD PARK

a screenplay
by
Julian Fellowes

based upon an idea
by
Robert Altman and Bob Balaban

SHOOTING SCRIPT: 02/20/01

Last Revision: 05/22/01

Pre-Title Sequence

1 EXT. THE COUNTESS OF TRENTHAM'S HOUSE. DAY. NOVEMBER. 1932.

It is a grey day. Mary Maceachran, a young Scottish lady's maid, watches a liveried chauffeur trying to start a green 1920s Daimler in front of a London house. The chauffeur, Merriman, climbs out with a crank handle which he fits and turns.

MERRIMAN
Just start, you filthy heap of scrap.

MARY
She'll hear you one of these days.

MERRIMAN
I don't care if she does.

MARY
Don't you just?

The motor catches and he stands. While the passenger seats are enclosed, the front, driving seat is open to the weather. Mary places a basket with a thermos glass and a sealed, tin sandwich container on the rear seat. As she does so, it begins to rain.

BUTLER (VO)
Mary? Merriman? Are you ready?

With a final check, she looks up to where a butler in a black morning coat waits.

MARY
Yes, Mr Burkett.

We can hardly hear his "Everything's ready, milady," nor can we see the face behind the veil of the figure who hurries down the steps. This is Constance, Countess of Trentham. Muffled in furs against the cold, she hurries into the waiting vehicle.

The titles run over the following sequence.

2 EXT. COUNTRY ROAD. DAY.

Merriman drives. Mary sits silently next to him, huddling into her coat. Unlike the passenger, the servants, in the roofless front seat, are exposed to the rain.

3 INT. CONSTANCE'S CAR. COUNTRY ROAD. DAY.

Gloved hands try lazily to open the thermos, give up immediately and reach for the polished brass speaking tube. The veiled indistinct mouth gives some instructions.

4 EXT. COUNTRY ROAD. DAY.

They pull over and the dripping maid gets out as a large Lagonda stops. It is bright with shining chrome. It looks like Tomorrow next to the Daimler's Yesterday. A man in the front passenger seat looks out helpfully. He speaks in a Californian accent.

WEISSMAN
Do you need any help? Are you O.K.?

The door is open now and, behind the maid, the indistinct passenger speaks.

CONSTANCE
Am I *what*?

MARY
We're quite all right. Thank you.

IVOR
Excuse me but… is that… Lady Trentham?

Constance does not answer.

IVOR (CONT'D)
You don't remember me… I'm William McCordle's cousin. Ivor Novello.

At this Mary gasps in recognition but Constance merely nods.

CONSTANCE
Of course.

IVOR
May I present a friend of mine from California, Morris Weissman? And –

Having indicated the American on the passenger side in front, he has turned to a very handsome young man sitting behind but, on second thoughts, he breaks off.

IVOR (CONT'D)
I was wondering if we were all headed in the same direction…

CONSTANCE
I dare say we might be.

IVOR
Well… if you're sure you don't need any help…

(CONTINUED)

4 CONTINUED:

Mary has opened the folding table for the refreshments. The other car drives away.

MARY
Was that *really* Ivor Novello?

CONSTANCE
Could we get on before I freeze to death?

The maid shuts the car door, climbs in and the journey continues. The credits end.

5 EXT. GOSFORD PARK. DAY.

The great house stands confidently in its park, proclaiming its social pre-eminence. As the car continues down the drive, it catches the attention of a beautiful woman who is cantering on her horse, Topaz. She wears jodphurs and a loosely tied neck scarf over her hacking jacket. This is Lady Sylvia McCordle, daughter of an earl and *doyenne* of Gosford. She digs in her heels and heads for the house.

As she arrives at the front steps, the Novello car is moving away to the side and Novello himself, with his companion, is being shepherded inside by the butler, Jennings. A footman (Arthur) holds an umbrella. With them is the owner of all he surveys, Sir William McCordle, bart, a rich *parvenu* and proud of it. In his arms he holds a wiry unattractive terrier The arrival of Constance makes him turn back.

WILLIAM
Constance. Welcome.

The visitor nods as Sylvia jumps down from her horse, tossing the reins back over its head. She gives her aunt a kiss.

CONSTANCE
If he has to call me by my christian name, why can't he make it "Aunt Constance"? I'm not the upstairs maid.

SYLVIA
You know what he's like.

CONSTANCE
I see he's still got that vile dog.

SYLVIA
It's so typical. The ones you hate live forever. Have you had a horrid journey?

5 CONTINUED:

CONSTANCE
Fairly horrid.

SYLVIA
You must be frozen. Come and have some tea.

Mary eyes the standing horse warily. With a snort, it shakes its head and, rather gingerly, she stretches out her hand to take the reins under the animal's chin. At once it starts to fidget and plunge. Sylvia looks across.

SYLVIA (CONT'D)
Leave him alone. He knows what to do.

The embarrassed maid drops the reins as a groom appears and leads the docile horse away. Mary, of course, does not know what to do.

Sylvia and her aunt start up the steps but we do not follow as they move off camera.

Jennings steps forward.

JENNINGS
Take the car round the back to unload it.

The car starts up and heads towards the side of the house. Still, Mary waits. Jennings looks over to the maid as he also starts to reclimb the front steps.

JENNINGS (CONT'D)
You'd better follow him. Mrs Wilson'll look after you.

A lone figure, she trudges off through the puddles, clutching the dressing case, as the car carrying the Stockbridge party sweeps up to the front.

6 INT. KITCHEN CORRIDOR. DAY.

Chaos reigns. Servants duck past the piled up trunks and cases. Valets and maids (Barnes and Sarah, joined later by Renee and Robert) struggle to check that none of their luggage has gone to the wrong rooms. Surveying it all, clipboard in hand, is Mrs Wilson, the house-keeper, an opaque woman in her middle years. Barnes, who is carrying a large flat, crested case approaches. She does not look up.

(CONTINUED)

6 CONTINUED:

MRS WILSON
Just leave everything in one pile, make sure it's properly labelled and it'll be taken up.

BARNES
These are the *guns*. Where's the gun room?

His voice could scarcely be more disdainful. She nods at a side corridor.

MRS WILSON
At the end on the left. You'll find the keeper, Mr Strutt, in there. He'll show you what to do.

BARNES
I know what to do.

He goes as Mary arrives timidly, sheltering behind a laden Merriman.

MRS WILSON
Yes?

MARY
Hello.

MERRIMAN
The Countess of Trentham.

Merriman has carried in the three smart cases. He knows the ropes. Mrs Wilson nods and checks her list, handing a label to the man.

MRS WILSON
Leave them over there by the luggage lift and tie this to the top one. You'll find the chauffeur, Mr Raikes, in the courtyard. He'll tell you where to put the car. You'll sleep in the stable block with the grooms.

He sets about the task, leaving Mary feeling more alone than ever.

MRS WILSON (CONT'D)
Her ladyship is in the Blue Damask Room. You'll be sharing with the Head Parlourmaid.
(MORE)

MRS WILSON (CONT'D)
She'll show you where everything is.
Elsie, this is Miss Trentham.

A young, uniformed maid, Elsie, turns at the sound of her name and comes near.

MARY
Excuse me, m'm, but… my name's Maceachran…

ELSIE
Not here it's not.

Mrs Wilson has moved away as Elsie takes Mary's case.

MARY
What about the jewels?

She indicates the dressing case still in her hand.

ELSIE
This way. George is in charge of the safe. He's the First Footman. And you want to watch where he puts his hands…

They turn another corner in the maze of service corridors that run beneath the house. At the door of the Butler's Silver Pantry, stands a supercilious figure in livery. Next to him, just inside the room, is a large wall safe. The iron door is open revealing a felt-lined closet, filled with laden shelves. George, the first footman, is receiving a case from another maid (Renee). Mary takes a key on a chain around her neck under her dress and opens the case, removing the jewel box which she is about to hand over.

ELSIE (CONT'D)
Have you got the ones for tonight?

MARY
Oh…

Mary unlocks the box. Inside are gleaming trays, each one with a complete parure of gems. She takes out a set of sapphires and puts them in the pocket of her coat.

ELSIE
Always take a separate box with the first night's jewels. Saves bother.

Mary nods, re-locking the box and handing it over to George who gives her a wink as he takes it. As they walk away, re-crossing the back hall, they almost collide with a tall stranger carrying a suitcase. Mrs Wilson arrives.

MRS WILSON
Elsie, this is Lord Stockbridge's valet. Show him the footmen's staircase, will you? And he'll need the ironing room.

She starts to leave. The new arrival turns to the two maids.

ROBERT
The name's Robert. Robert Parks.

This seems to halt the retreating Mrs Wilson. Robert looks at her enquiringly.

MRS WILSON
I meant to say you'll be sharing with Mr Weissman's man. You could have gone up together but I don't know where he's got to.

Other business claims her. Elsie sighs. They might as well get on with it.

ELSIE
Has his lordship's luggage gone up?

ROBERT
Supposedly. He's in the Tapestry Room wherever that is… Oh well, here, we go again.

But Mary cannot return his casual pleasantry. Instead she half whispers.

MARY
That's just it. I've never done a house-party before. Not properly…

ROBERT
You'll be all right.

Elsie, above them on the back stair, has overheard.

ELSIE
How d'you manage to be taken on as a countess's lady's maid if you didn't 'ave no experience?

MARY
She wants to train me. She said she didn't care about experience.

6 CONTINUED: (4)

ELSIE
She didn't want to pay for it, you mean.

7 INT. KITCHEN. DAY.

A handsome face displays the brilliant smile of Henry Denton, Morris Weissman's valet. At the long table, the cook, Mrs Croft, is working on a tray of quail. The senior kitchen maid, Bertha, slices carrots and the junior, Ellen, slowly turns an ice-cream churn. They ogle the visitor who speaks in a Scottish accent.

MRS CROFT
Get on with your work. Yes?

HENRY
I just –

But before he can say more, Mrs Wilson spies him from the corridor and enters.

MRS WILSON
Ah, Mr Weissman, there you are.

MRS CROFT
*I'm* dealing with this. What is it, Mr Weissman?

The dislike between the two women is almost tangible.

HENRY
Well, to start with my name is Denton. Henry Denton.

MRS WILSON
You are here as valet to Mr Weissman. That means you will be known, below stairs, as Mr Weissman for the duration of your stay. You'll find we keep to the old customs. It avoids confusion.

He would answer back but decides against it.

HENRY
It's about Mr Weissman's diet –

MRS WILSON AND MRS CROFT
Yes?

7 CONTINUED:

HENRY
He's a vegetarian.

MRS CROFT
A what?

HENRY
A vegetarian. He doesn't eat meat. He eats fish but not meat.

MRS CROFT
Well, I never.

HENRY
I'm sorry if it's inconvenient.

MRS CROFT
Well, it's not very convenient, I must say. Doesn't eat meat? He's come for a shooting party and he doesn't eat meat?

HENRY
Mr Weissman doesn't intend to shoot. I think he just wants to walk out with them. Get a bit of air.

MRS CROFT
*Get a bit of air?*

MRS WILSON
Thank you. We'll make the necessary adjustments. Now, if you'd like to get one of the servants to take you upstairs... Mr Weissman is in the Mulgrave Room and you'll be sharing with Lord Stockbridge's valet.

Henry nods his thanks and walks out of the room watched by Mrs Croft.

MRS CROFT
He's very full of himself, I must say. Doesn't eat meat!

MRS WILSON
Come along, Mrs Croft. We don't want to be thought unsophisticated, do we? Mr Weissman is an American. They do things differently there.

She goes, leaving Mrs Croft seething.

(CONTINUED)

7 CONTINUED: (2)

MRS CROFT
I'll give her 'unsophisticated'!

Her assistants giggle but their response does not please the cook.

MRS CROFT (CONT'D)
What are you gawping at? Those are no good. I said 'julienne.' And Ellen that is ice-cream you are churning not concrete. Calm down.

8 INT. ELSIE'S ATTIC ROOM. DAY.

This is a simple, plainly furnished room with two beds. Mary hangs up her coat then opens the valise on the bed. She unbuttons her wet travelling dress and takes a black frock from the case then a cap and a frilly, black apron. Elsie watches her.

ELSIE
I thought ladies' maids never wore aprons.

MARY
Her ladyship used to have a French maid who wore a black one like this. She thinks it's got a bit of style.

ELSIE
I bet she does. And I'll bet she took it out of your wages, too.

MARY
She likes to have everything just so.

Elsie rolls her eyes.

ELSIE
Don't they all?

Behind Elsie's bed are various pictures of movie stars, postcards or cut from magazines. Mary goes over to the collection to admire it. She points.

MARY
That's him!

This is surprising as the picture is principally of Garbo with a man behind her.

(CONTINUED)

8 CONTINUED:

ELSIE
Who'd you mean?

MARY
Ivor Novello. He passed us on the road today, on his way here, and he spoke to me. Well… he spoke to her ladyship but I answered…

ELSIE
I only cut it out for Garbo. I prefer the American stars. I think they've got more oomph.

MARY
Go on. Is he really Sir William's cousin? Imagine having a film star in the family. Lady Sylvia must be thrilled.

ELSIE
I don't think.

MARY
Why wouldn't she be?

ELSIE
Because she's a snobbish cow. Because she looks down on anyone who got to the top with brains and hard work. Just like she looks down on her husband. Except when it's time to foot the bills. Then she's got her hand out all right.

MARY
What was her family, then?

ELSIE
What you'd expect. Toffee-nosed and useless. Her father was the Earl of Carton which sounds good except he didn't have a pot to piss in.

MARY
What's she like to work for?

ELSIE
Horrible but he… he's O.K…. Come on. We'd better get cracking.

9 INT. KITCHEN CORRIDOR. DAY.

Probert, Sir William's valet, is carrying a boiled-front dress shirt past Mrs Wilson.

PROBERT
Can't think why I'm so behind today. The gong hasn't gone, has it?

MRS WILSON
Oh no, you've plenty of time yet.

PROBERT
'Cos you know what a fuss he's in when he's playing Mine Host...I think I'll go and get him a paper if there's time...

This last is to himself as he hurries on. Mrs Wilson notices something in the corridor that displeases her.

MRS WILSON
George? What are you up to? Hasn't Mr Jennings given you anything to do?

GEORGE
I'm just going to help him with the tea. Then I'm to finish the table with Arthur.

MRS WILSON
Well get on with it then.

With a movement suspiciously like the discarding of a cigarette, he nods, starting up the service stair that leads to the main house.

10 INT. UPSTAIRS HALL AND CORRIDOR. DAY.

Emerging from the green baize door, George crosses a magnificent staircase hall. As he goes, he hears a whispered, angry exchange although he cannot detect the source.

MAN (VO)
What do you mean "no"? You promised!

YOUNG WOMAN (VO)
I never promised! I said I'd do my best… Anyway, I'm going to ask him tonight.

(CONTINUED)

10 CONTINUED:

MAN (VO)
You'd bloody well better! What –

This is provoked by George stepping from the rug to the polished floor. The speaker, The Hon. Freddie Nesbitt, emerges. His anxiety dissolves at the sight of a footman.

FREDDIE
It's all right. It's nobody.

He is joined by a young woman, Isobel McCordle.

ISOBEL
You shouldn't sneak up on people like that.

GEORGE
Sorry, Miss Isobel.

The camera stays with the servant as the others walk away, their voices fading.

FREDDIE (VO)
Do you really think you'll have a chance to talk to him tonight?

ISOBEL (VO)
Oh, do stop going on about it.

FREDDIE (VO)
That's all very fine but why the hell do you think I've come here?

George turns the handle of the saloon door, without knocking, and goes silently in.

11 INT. SALOON/LIBRARY. DAY.

Sitting at a table, surrounded by the evidence of a large tea, are Constance Trentham, Morris Weissman, and Mabel Nesbitt. Ivor is holding court, enthralling Mabel with Hollywood gossip. The others sprawl around the room, balancing plates and cups with magazines and cigarettes as they drawl and chatter. Jennings presides over the teapot. George, followed by Isobel, Freddie and the Stockbridges, enters and takes his position by the door as Lt. Commander Anthony and Lady Lavinia Meredith approach the tea table. He is ex-navy, she is Sylvia's sister. Their tone is urgent and could not be overheard - except possibly by the butler.

ANTHONY
What do you mean "leave it?"

(CONTINUED)

LAVINIA
I just meant let it come up naturally.
Don't steer the conversation. It makes
you sound so desperate.

ANTHONY
Well, I am fucking desperate.

They cross the room to sit down, passing the tea-table.

MABEL
What's Greta Garbo really like? Did
you get to know her?

IVOR
I did. As a matter of fact, she's
coming to stay with me next month.

Mabel gasps. Her shop-girl awe reassures Ivor but it irritates
Constance.

CONSTANCE
Tell me, how much longer do you think
you'll go on making films?

IVOR
That depends how much longer the
public wants to see me in them.

CONSTANCE
I expect it's hard to know when it's
time to throw in the towel...What a
pity about that last one of yours.
What was it? "The Dodger"?

IVOR
"The Lodger"

CONSTANCE
It must be *so* disappointing...When
something just *flops* like that. After
all the hard work.

IVOR
Yes, I suppose it is rather
disappointing.

Sylvia arrives at the table.

WEISSMAN
You have some beautiful antiques, Lady
Sylvia. Real museum quality.
(MORE)

11 CONTINUED: (2)

WEISSMAN (CONT'D)
I'm interested: How much would a picture like that set you back?

SYLVIA
I hope you've all got everything you need.

She shares the moment with Constance before walking back towards the open library door where McCordle is sitting at a work table covered with gun tools and a pistol feeding his terrier, Pip. Keeping him company is Louisa Stockbridge.

LOUISA
Who's the funny little American?

WILLIAM
Morris Weissman? A friend of Ivor's. He makes films in Hollywood. Ivor asked if he could bring him and I didn't see why not. I thought he might be interested in shooting but...

LOUISA
Never mind. He adds to the glamour of the gathering. I didn't expect anything half as exotic.

During this, William goes to pour two whiskies. He splashes a little soda into them. Nearby a door set into the books opens and Probert appears. He is surprised to find the room occupied.

PROBERT
I beg your pardon, Sir. I just thought I'd take the Times up with me. In case you want to read it when you dress.

WILLIAM
Good thinking, Probert.

As the valet looks for the paper, William hands the drink to Louisa but she shakes her head.

LOUISA
Not for me. Far too early. And you know I never drink whisky.

WILLIAM
Nonsense. Come on. Drink up. It's good for you.

(CONTINUED)

11 CONTINUED: (3)

LOUISA
Really, Bill. You're such a bad influence. Don't blame me if I pass out at dinner.

But she takes the drink and sips it as the valet takes the paper and leaves.

WILLIAM
I don't know how impressed your husband is with our Showbiz folk. He looks as if he's being forced to share a railway sleeper with a garage mechanic.

LOUISA
I'm afraid he only feels safe with his own kind.

WILLIAM
Poor old Raymond.

LOUISA
If you think he's dull you should've met his father. He made Raymond look like Buster Keaton.

12 INT. KITCHEN CORRIDOR. EVE.

Mary carries three evening frocks while Elsie carries one. She holds it up.

ELSIE
Mrs Nesbitt. She's only got this one with her. Says her husband rushed her when she was packing.

MARY
Do you always look after visitors if they don't have a maid?

ELSIE
Sometimes Dorothy helps. Though why Mrs Wilson makes the Still Room Maid do it beats me...I think it's just to annoy Mrs Croft.

MARY
Which one does Dorothy answer to?

(CONTINUED)

12 CONTINUED:

ELSIE
Both. And she's worked off her feet. But then *I* do Miss Isobel as well...Here we are.

She opens a door and goes in.

13 INT. IRONING AND SEWING ROOM. EVE.

In the centre are several ironing boards. Barnes, Robert, Sarah and Renee are in there working. Robert brushes glaze on an evening waistcoat as he irons it.

ELSIE
You found it, then?

She smiles at Robert. Then points to a cupboard.

ELSIE (CONT'D)
This one's yours.

MARY
Thanks.

ROBERT
What's your name?

MARY
I think here I'm called Trentham…

ROBERT
No. I meant your real name?

MARY
Mary. Mary Maceachran.

ROBERT
Blimey. What does her ladyship call you?

MARY
Well, it should be Maceachran. That's what my mother says. Now I'm a lady's maid. But she can't pronounce it so she calls me Mary.

ROBERT
I don't blame her.

Elsie irons with contempt.

(CONTINUED)

13 CONTINUED:

ELSIE
Machine-made lace.

BARNES
Hark at her.

ELSIE
I hate cheap clothes. Twice the work and they never look any good.

RENEE
What d'you expect from a woman without her own maid?

SARAH
Lady Lavinia always says a woman who travels with no maid has lost her self-respect. She calls it "giving in."

ELSIE
I don't have a maid and I haven't "given in."

SARAH
That's different.

ELSIE
Why?

BARNES
Yes, why is it different, Sarah?

SARAH
Miss Morse to you.

14 INT. KITCHEN CORRIDOR. EVE.

Henry is carrying some clothes and a pair of stout shoes. As he goes, he opens every door and looks inside… He marvels at the complexities of the still room, then at the larders and so on. He jumps at the sound of a voice. It is Arthur, the Second Footman.

ARTHUR
Can I help you?

HENRY
I er… I was looking for the brushing room… I thought I'd give Mr Weissman's tweeds a going-over for tomorrow.

14 CONTINUED:

ARTHUR
I'll show you... Here y'are.

He opens a door and Henry goes in.

15 INT. BRUSHING ROOM. EVE.

There is a covered table with every type of brush on it. Lewis, Sylvia's maid, is working on the hacking jacket. Henry puts down the shoes and lays out the tweeds.

ARTHUR
The boot room's next door...Do you really live in Hollywood?

HENRY
I do.

ARTHUR
But how did you get there? I mean, where did you start from?

HENRY
Where do you think? Scotland.

This answer is not quite satisfying to Arthur. He looks at Lewis. Then he presses on.

ARTHUR
Were you always in service? Or did you ever think of trying to get into films? I wanted to be an actor once...when I was little...

HENRY
Was that a bell?

LEWIS
It's not the dressing gong, is it?

ARTHUR
Can't be time for them to change yet, surely.

He goes off to investigate as Henry tries different brushes to suit the tweed.

15A INT. RED SALOON. EVE.

Tea is nearly finished. Jennings hands an empty tray to George.

(CONTINUED)

15A CONTINUED:

JENNINGS
Its nearly time for the gong. If they don't want any more, take their cups and plates. If they do, don't give them much.

George walks towards the sofa on the left of the fire-place.

RAYMOND
Sylvia, I mean it. There mustn't be any nonsense.

SYLVIA
I don't know what you're talking about.

Sylvia, without her hacking jacket but still in jodphurs, speaks to her other brother-in-law, Raymond Stockbridge. With George on camera, we hear them before we see them. Raymond sits reading a magazine but it is clear that something has set him on edge.

SYLVIA (CONT'D)
Have you done a lot of shooting this year?

RAYMOND
Quite a lot.

GEORGE
Are you finished, your ladyship? Or would you like some more tea?

SYLVIA
All finished, thank you, George. So is Lord Stockbridge.

He starts to clear as she looks across at the silent peer.

SYLVIA (CONT'D)
Does Louisa always go out with you?

RAYMOND
Usually.

SYLVIA
How good she is...It bores me stiff, I'm afraid. And William's such a rotten shot, he doesn't really like anyone standing with him. I try and duck out of it. Particularly if it's Scotland.

RAYMOND
I'm very fond of Scotland...

He speaks without looking up as George takes his tray and us over to the table.

CONSTANCE
But what a waste! If *you're* not shooting either, then they'll only be six! William? Isn't that a shame...

She addresses William who stands in the library doorway with Louisa. Anthony makes a move to speak to him but William's words deter him.

WILLIAM
It doesn't matter...I'm going up to change.

CONSTANCE
Well, I *am* surprised. Normally anything to do with shooting or those wretched guns is sacrosanct. What is your secret, I wonder?

Ivor drifts over to Sylvia.

IVOR
I am sorry about that. I should have made it clear. Stupid of me.

SYLVIA
Nonsense. It's William's fault. He just has this idea that all Americans sleep with guns under their pillows.

IVOR
So they do. But they're more for each other than for killing birds.

She laughs as Raymond looks up from his reading.

RAYMOND
Remind me, how are you related to William exactly?

IVOR
Our mothers were first cousins.

RAYMOND
Really? I don't know that I ever met William's mother. Didn't she do something rather original?

George crosses back to the now clear tea-table.

IVOR
She was a teacher. So was mine.

RAYMOND
Oh? Well, of course that's marvellous, isn't it?

Back at the table, Constance is ingratiating herself with her neighbour.

CONSTANCE
Sylvia's *so* clever. She always finds such wonderful servants. I don't know how she manages. I'm breaking in a new maid and I'm simply worn out with it. There's nothing more exhausting, is there?

MABEL
I don't have a lady's maid.

She gives the information flatly but Constance remains light. Sylvia has given up on Raymond and come to look for a cigarette in a box on the tea-table.

CONSTANCE
I was just telling dear Mabel here about my new maid. Honestly, for all the help I have to give her, she should be paying *me*...

SYLVIA
She does look rather young.

Constance drops her voice so that only Sylvia (and George) can hear.

CONSTANCE
Well of course what she is, my dear, is *wonderfully* cheap.

She laughs softly with her niece. During all this, George has removed the cloth, and folded the tea-table.

16 INT. IRONING AND SEWING ROOM. DAY.

SARAH
I s'pose Old Mother Trentham'll have her begging bowl out while she's here.

RENEE
She won't be bothering your employer. That's for sure.

MARY
What d'you mean? Why not?

ELSIE
'Cos Lady Lavinia Meredith hasn't a penny to bless herself with.

BARNES
And who's fault is that?

SARAH
There's nothing wrong with the Commander. He's just been a bit unfortunate.

BARNES
I'll say. I think he's pathetic.

SARAH
Then why don't you hand in your notice?

RENEE
Well, the other two sisters fell on their feet. 'Course, it helps that they're good-looking.

MARY
Lady Sylvia's lovely.

ELSIE
Do you think so?

SARAH
She might have done a bit better for herself, really.

ELSIE
I beg your pardon. Lord Carton was determined to get Sir William for either of the two eldest. I was told he could have had his pick.

(CONTINUED)

16 CONTINUED:

MARY
Why was Lord Carton so keen?

BARNES
Why d'you think? Who d'you suppose pays for him to swan around Biarritz for six months a year. Come to that, who keeps Ma Trentham in stockings and gin? Old Money Bags, that's who.

ELSIE
I think it's disgusting. The way they use him. Especially when they all look down on him 'cos he's made it himself. None of them have got the brains to make the price of a packet of tea.

MRS WILSON
Have you finished, Elsie?

She is in the doorway.

ELSIE
Nearly, Mrs Wilson. I've just got these cuffs to do.

MRS WILSON
When you're ready make your way to the Servants' Hall. We dine after the guests are dressed and before we serve dinner.

She goes. Barnes follows, saying,

BARNES
Here we go. Yes sir, no sir, three bags full, sir.

MARY
What's Lord Stockbridge like?

ROBERT
He thinks he's God Almighty but they all do.

17 INT. DINING-ROOM. EVE.

A beautiful and complicated table-setting fills the screen with six glasses of different shapes and sizes, and silver cutlery ranged sideways out from a place mat supporting a folded napkin.

(CONTINUED)

17 CONTINUED:

On the right, among the spoons and knives is a single fork while all the other forks are on the left. A hand enters the frame and takes it up.

HENRY (VO)
Why does this fork go on the right?

Henry is examining it. Arthur, wearing green baize gloves for moving silver, takes it back, spits on it, rubs it lightly and replaces it.

ARTHUR
Because they eat their fish with two of them. One in each hand.

HENRY
Why's that then?

ARTHUR
Search me.

George enters. He carries a tray holding some full, red wine decanters.

GEORGE
What are you doing here?

HENRY
Just looking around.

George unloads the tray onto the sideboard then takes a ruler out of a drawer and starts to measure the exact distance between the place settings.

GEORGE
Mr Jennings'll be up in a minute. If I were you, I'd go and 'look around' somewhere else.

HENRY
Whatever you say.

With a smile, he leaves. Arthur waits until the door shuts.

ARTHUR
There's something funny about that bloke...

GEORGE
His accent for a start. Where do you -

17 CONTINUED: (2)

JENNINGS
Are you finished? What about Lord Rupert Standish and Mr Blond?

He stands in the other door. Frowning, he moves an entire place setting slightly to the left.

GEORGE
Her ladyship said not to lay for them. The stuff's ready if they get here in time. We can stick two more places on in a jiffy.

JENNINGS
When they arrive, you'll be dressing Mr Blond, Arthur. George, you'll have Lord Rupert. If they're very late, they can change by themselves. You can tidy up when they're downstairs. Is Mr Nesbitt settled?

GEORGE
I'll go up and finish him off now.

ARTHUR
And Mr Novello?

JENNINGS
Mr Weissman's man will attend to him. Right. As soon as you're done, join me in the drawing-room for the drinks.

He goes. George folds up the ruler and puts it away.

GEORGE
What's the matter with you?

ARTHUR
Nothing… only I thought I'd be doing Mr Novello, that's all.

GEORGE
And now you won't see him in his under-drawers? Never mind. Better luck next time.

Arthur attempts to conceal his furious blushing.

18 INT. NOVELLO BEDROOM. EVE.

Henry is tidying things while Ivor stands in white tie and tails before a pier glass.

18 CONTINUED:

IVOR
So, how's it going? Are you enjoying yourself?

HENRY
Very much. Are you, sir?

19 INT. TRENTHAM BEDROOM. EVE.

Constance, wearing the blue dress we saw Mary ironing and the sapphires, is sitting in front of her looking glass. Mary arranges a small tiara in her mistress's hair.

CONSTANCE
Rather a mixed bag… That Mr Weissman's very odd. Apparently he's in films. He directs something called "The Charlie Chan Mysteries." Or does he produce them? I never know the difference.

MARY
Really? I enjoy those, milady.

Constance lights a cigarette. She isn't interested in Mary's movie-going.

CONSTANCE
I suppose it's fun to have a film star staying but there's always so little to talk about after the first flush of recognition. And why has Freddie Nesbitt brought that awful, common wife of his? Isobel only asked him because a gun dropped out and that's no excuse to inflict her on us all. And I'm told he's been sacked from his bank now. Thank heaven he's a younger son... So, what's the gossip in the servants' hall?

MARY
Nothing, really, milady.

But Constance knows better than that as she puffs away.

CONSTANCE
Nonsense. Out with it.

MARY
Well… is it true that Sir William could have married Lady Stockbridge? If he'd wanted to?

(CONTINUED)

CONSTANCE
Is that what they're saying?

MARY
Only that Lord Carton was after Sir William for one of them and he didn't care which…

CONSTANCE
What would you say if I told you they cut cards for him?

MARY
What? They didn't, did they?

For a moment Constance relishes the shock on her maid's face.

CONSTANCE
Of course not. Now, tomorrow morning I'll breakfast in bed and get straight up into the tweeds. What shirt have you brought?

MARY
The pink with the green check.

CONSTANCE
Oh no, dear. Quite wrong. Always something very plain for country sports. The one I had on today will do.

MARY
But it's soiled.

CONSTANCE
Well? You can wash it, can't you… God, I hate shooting. Why does one have to do these things?

MARY
Couldn't you stay indoors? Lady Sylvia wouldn't mind.

CONSTANCE
Maybe not but *he* would. He's terribly touchy. Worse since they made him a baronet. Now he thinks he's the last Plantagenet and takes offence accordingly.

19 CONTINUED: (2)

She turns a searching eye on her image in the glass, smearing rouge into her cheek.

20 INT. MCCORDLE DRESSING ROOM. EVE.

Probert is putting the finishing touches to Sir William's evening dress. The new baronet looks at the reflection of himself. His dog also checks out the final effect.

WILLIAM
And you really don't think a handkerchief?

PROBERT
*No*, sir.

McCordle reluctantly accepts his valet's judgement. Probert (and the camera) crosses the door at the moment it opens and Sylvia appears, her hard beauty accentuated by the superb cut of her clothes. When she speaks, it is difficult to mask her indifference.

SYLVIA
I'm going down. Lewis said you wanted me.

WILLIAM (VO)
Who's next to me at dinner?

SYLVIA
You know who. Aunt Constance and Lavinia.

WILLIAM
Why do I have to have the old trout the whole bloody time? Why can't I have Louisa?

SYLVIA
Do you really want me to explain the Table of Precedence now? Or can it wait?

Her voice is dripping with sarcasm.

WILLIAM (VO)
Who gives a shit about precedence?

Probert walks over to put something into a tall-boy near Sylvia in time for us to see her shrug, speaking wearily as she would to a tiresome child.

(CONTINUED)

SYLVIA
You rage when people look down on you and then you insist on behaving like a vulgar ignoramus.

Her contemptuous words have their effect. This is how she controls him.

WILLIAM (VO)
Has Constance asked you for any money yet?

The camera has followed Probert as he continues to tidy the dressing-room. Now he takes a crested, ivory clothes brush from a tall-boy and returns to Sir William.

SYLVIA
No.

WILLIAM
Raymond says she's been complaining that her allowance isn't big enough. I've a good mind to stop it altogether.

SYLVIA
I thought it was settled for her lifetime.

WILLIAM
Says who?

His manner is bullying and unpleasant but Sylvia is uninterested.

SYLVIA
Will that be all, sir?

Probert restrains a smile as he carries the clothes brush back to the dressing-table.

WILLIAM (VO)
I wish Anthony wasn't here. Try and make sure he doesn't get me on my own, can you?

SYLVIA (VO)
Why?

WILLIAM (VO)
I'm pulling out of his scheme.

20 CONTINUED: (2)

Probert brings the camera back to them and he stands, waiting to speak.

SYLVIA
Oh? Have you told him?

WILLIAM
No. And I'm not going to if I can help it. Louisa thought I should do it next week. Then he can sob in private. Spare Lavinia's blushes.

SYLVIA
Far be it from me to contradict Louisa… Poor little Anthony. I thought he was looking unusually pathetic at tea...Get away from me.

She shoves Pip off her foot as Probert bows.

PROBERT
Will there be anything else, sir?

WILLIAM
No, thank you, Probert.

21 INT. GALLERY. EVE.

As Probert emerges, Elsie is coming down the gallery looking harrassed.

PROBERT
Everything all right, girl?

ELSIE
Honestly, I don't know how I'll manage. She's forgotten her hairpins. She hasn't packed the right shoes… I'm making bricks without straw, Mr Probert. Really I am.

Mary appears, carrying the dirty shirt.

ELSIE (CONT'D)
I don't suppose you've got any hairpins to spare, have you?

MARY
Hang on a minute.

She rummages in a *chatelaine* and finds a few. Muttering thanks, Elsie hurries away.

(CONTINUED)

21 CONTINUED:

PROBERT
On your way down? I'll take you.

MARY
I thought I'd just nip up to my room for a minute...only...

PROBERT
Yes?

MARY
Which way *is* my room?

22 INT. GALLERY. EVE.

George is emerging from the Nesbitts' bedroom as Elsie arrives.

ELSIE
Is he done?

He nods, raising his eyebrows, and goes. She reaches for the door handle when there is a movement at the end of the gallery. William and his dog are both looking at her. With a secret smile, Elsie returns his gaze before she opens the door.

23 INT. NESBITT BEDROOM. EVE.

Mabel is at the dressing table and, for a moment, it seems that Freddie has his wife's wrist in his fist. He swings round and, if he did have hold of her, he releases it.

ELSIE
I've got some pins, madam. From Lady Trentham's maid.

FREDDIE
We should be downstairs already.

MABEL
You go on. I'll be as quick as I can.

FREDDIE
Try and make her look respectable.

He says this to the maid and goes without a comment from either woman. They stare at each other through the glass. Mabel with her pasty face and lank hair looks terrible.

MABEL
Well, there's no harm in trying.

24 INT. DRAWING-ROOM. EVE.

Jennings carries a salver with two martini glasses to Ivor who is playing the grand piano. Is it "I Can Give You The Starlight"? He and Weissman take the drinks.

WEISSMAN
Thank you, Mr Jennings.

JENNINGS
Just Jennings, sir.

WEISSMAN
Then thank you, Jennings.

JENNINGS
I'll clear the piano for you, sir.

He lifts the photographs and albums that litter the closed lid of the grand as Sylvia approaches. Ivor stands but she makes him play. Behind her, the others drift in.

SYLVIA
Jennings, can I have a martini when you've done that? Oh, don't get up. Go on. Please. What is it? I don't believe I know it.

IVOR
Nothing… an idea I've been fiddling with…

WEISSMAN
By the way, Jennings. I've a telephone call booked. For California. If you could let me know as soon as they get through.

JENNINGS
Very good, sir.

SYLVIA
I can't imagine how one could ever invent a tune… How do you start?

IVOR
It's rather hard to say exactly.

SYLVIA
Well I think it's too clever for any words.

(CONTINUED)

24 CONTINUED:

She strolls back to join the others. Weissman watches her as Jennings finally lifts the lid of the piano, filling the room with music. He starts back to the drinks table.

WEISSMAN
How do you manage these people?

IVOR
You forget. I make my living impersonating them. What does he want?

Across the room, Henry has come in. He lingers by the door as Jennings approaches

JENNINGS
Can I help you?

HENRY
You know... I really enjoy the way you do things, Mr Jennings.

JENNINGS
I beg your pardon.

Weissman has left the piano and crossed the room.

WEISSMAN
What is it, Henry?

HENRY
Nothing. I just wanted to be sure you have everything you need. Sir.

WEISSMAN
Yes. Thank you.

Henry goes, leaving Jennings completely bewildered. Weissman acknowledges him.

WEISSMAN (CONT'D)
It's so good to find a servant these days who takes an interest.

25 INT. SERVANTS' HALL. EVE.

A table is laid for dinner with a nervous boy ready to serve. All the indoor servants except the kitchen staff are here including two housemaids, May and Janet. Merriman nods at Mary. Jennings enters with George and Arthur.

DOROTHY
Everything satisfactory, Mr Jennings?

(CONTINUED)

25 CONTINUED:

JENNINGS
Yes, thank you, Dorothy. They have their drinks. We can take our leisure for half an hour, I think.

At the head of the table, he looks at Renee who stands on his right. His brow darkens.

JENNINGS (CONT'D)
What's this?

DOROTHY
I did tell her, Mr Jennings.

RENEE
I believe this is my place, Mr Jennings.

JENNINGS
Oh? Since when did a baroness outrank a countess? Or is that some foreign custom you've picked up on your travels?

Renee purses her lips but says nothing.

JENNINGS (CONT'D)
Miss Trentham? Would you like to come and take the seat of honour?

But Mary does not recognise her 'name'. He repeats it and Arthur nudges her.

MARY
I'm all right here, Mr Jennings, thank you.

DOROTHY
Go on. Don't keep him waiting.

Jennings stands. Mary, blushing, moves to his right hand side, displacing Renee who moves to Jennings's left but even that does not satisfy him.

JENNINGS
Miss Meredith, you may come to my left if you please.

As Renee stalks down the table, Mary turns queryingly to George. He whispers.

GEORGE
Her mistress married a baron so she lost her rank as an earl's daughter. Renee always tries to catch Mr Jennings out but no one can.

LEWIS
Naturally I'm nothing when there's visitors in the house. Never mind. I'm used to it.

No one pays her any attention as the housekeeper, Mrs Wilson, makes her own stately entrance and takes her place at the far end between Robert and Probert.

MRS WILSON
Good evening, Mr Jennings.

Jennings nods, says Grace and they sit. The boy holds a plate for Mrs Wilson and then the butler. Unlike upstairs, they pass vegetable dishes across the table.

JENNINGS
Right. Start when you get it. No time for loitering.

HENRY
Can I ask a question?

JENNINGS
Certainly, Mr Weissman. How can we help?

HENRY
I just wondered. How many people here had parents in service? And was that why they chose to go into it?

JENNINGS
That's an interesting point and one I can't answer. All those of you whose parents were in service raise your hand.

Most hands go up. We hear "not both of them" or "just for a bit, before they married," "I s'pose they expected me to," and so on. Only Dorothy, Barnes and Robert are left.

JENNINGS (CONT'D)
Not you, Dorothy?

25 CONTINUED: (3)

DOROTHY
My dad was a farmer, Mr Jennings. A
tenant of Lord Carton's.

JENNINGS
Mr Meredith?

BARNES
Factory hands. Both of them. And if
you ask me, they were better off.

HENRY
What about you, Mr Stockbridge?

Robert looks up. Something in this attracts Mrs Wilson's attention. He shrugs.

GEORGE
What's the matter? Don't you know?

ROBERT
Yes I know. I know what both of them
did as a matter of fact. But it didn't
have no effect on me. On my choice.

MRS WILSON

Why is that?

ROBERT
Because I grew up in an orphanage.

This wrong foots the company. Jennings quickly pulls a veil over matters.

JENNINGS
Thank you, Mr Weissman. For giving us
something to think about… I must
compliment Bertha on this stew. And
Mrs Croft on the choice of the beef,
of course. It's delicious.

Mary now has George on her other side. She whispers to him.

MARY
Where is Mrs Croft?

GEORGE
Always eats with her own staff.

(CONTINUED)

MARY
Does she take her pudding to Mrs Wilson's room? Our cook does that.

GEORGE
Not likely. She wouldn't set foot in there if her life depended on it. They hate each other.

JENNINGS
Something amusing, Miss Trentham? Can we share it?

Mary is saved by the arrival of Lady Sylvia McCordle. In her couture clothes and jewels, she is an enchanted creature from a fairy kingdom. The company jumps up.

SYLVIA
I am so sorry to disturb you all but a major crisis has arisen… I've just learned that Mr Weissman doesn't eat meat. Is it a Jewish thing? I always thought that was pork and prawns...But the point is: What *are* we to do? I can't tell Mrs Croft. I simply don't dare.

MRS WILSON
Everything's under control, your ladyship. Mr Weissman's valet informed me as soon as they arrived. We've prepared a special version of the soup, he can eat the hors d'oevres and the fish and we'll do Welsh Rabbit for the game course. I'm not sure about the entree but we'll think of something.

Sylvia's response is not as warm as it might be.

SYLVIA
Thank you, Mrs Wilson. Of course you're ten steps ahead. Which one of you is Mr Weissman's valet?

HENRY
I am, your ladyship.

Sylvia turns to deliver some patronising *bon mot* but she is absolutely arrested by the man's beauty. For a moment, she simply stares.

25 CONTINUED: (5)

SYLVIA
Are you, indeed? Heavens… well… thank you for being so efficient. Please don't let me interrupt you further.

She hurries away and they sit, dazed. George looks across at Henry with a wink.

GEORGE
You're all set, then.

A few junior servants giggle which does not amuse Mr Jennings one bit.

JENNINGS
Yes, George?

GEORGE
Nothing, Mr Jennings.

They transfer their attention to their plates.

26 EXT. KITCHEN COURT. NIGHT.

Mary, carrying a cup of tea, is walking across the courtyard towards the garages for the visitors' cars. We can see Merriman there working on Constance's car. There is a sound from the shadows. Bertha is sitting by herself, smoking.

MARY
You gave me a turn. I didn't see you there. Aren't you cold?

BERTHA
It feels good to be cold after a day in that kitchen.

Mary walks on until Merriman comes towards her.

MARY
I thought you could do with this.

MERRIMAN
That's kind, love. How are you getting on?

Before Mary can answer, they are interrupted by the arrival of an open roadster which sweeps in, all headlights and bright colour. It pulls to a halt and two young men, Lord Rupert Standish and Jeremy Blond, hop out.

(CONTINUED)

26 CONTINUED:

RUPERT
Can we get in this way?

MARY
Wouldn't you do better round the front, sir?

JEREMY
Exactly what I said.

RUPERT
The thing is we've got bags and guns and everything and neither of us has a man to carry them. I thought it made more sense to bring them to the back door. If I give you the keys perhaps someone can sort it out.

MARY
Of course.

As she stands back to allow the men into the house, something makes Jeremy turn. Bertha is watching them, smoking as she leans against the outside wall.

27 OMITTED

28 OMITTED

29 INT. SERVERY. NIGHT.

Dorothy and Janet tend a serving table, stacking plates and setting out clean ones from the heating cupboard. George passes with a dish of partridges, helping himself to a taste as he goes into the dining-room. Elsie arrives and starts to follow him.

DOROTHY
You can't go in there when you're not serving. What would Mr Jennings say?

ELSIE
Keep your hair on. It so happens I've got a message for your precious Mr Jennings.

30 INT. DINING-ROOM. NIGHT.

The party is at table. Because they are twelve, William sits at one end and Raymond

(CONTINUED)

30 CONTINUED:

at the other. George holds the dish for Constance on William's right. Arthur waits with a tray of game crisps, breadcrumbs, bread sauce and gravy.

CONSTANCE
I was wondering if I could have a word with you. Alone. After dinner.

WILLIAM
I don't think I should leave my guests, do you…

He leans down to feed Pip who sits beneath his chair.

CONSTANCE
You'll make that dog sick.

Weissman is talking to Louisa.

WEISSMAN
Of course I'm going out with them. Ivor's promised to look after me.

LOUISA
Ivor's going with you?

WEISSMAN
Certainly. He says he's looking forward to a good walk.

LOUISA
Is he? Doesn't sound very like Ivor. He normally stays in bed and comes out with the ladies for luncheon.

WEISSMAN
Well, he wants to show me how it all works.

Before she can respond to this, a dish is brought by Arthur to Weissman's left side.

LOUISA
Welsh Rabbit? Is that a vegetarian game course?

Freddie is on Sylvia's left.

FREDDIE
It was just a misunderstanding.

(CONTINUED)

SYLVIA
Oh? Aunt Constance seemed to think it was more serious than that.

FREDDIE
Only because she got her version from my father.

On her right, Raymond eats in silence. There is a crack of thunder as she turns to him.

SYLVIA
Ivor and Mabel are talking in the wrong direction so you'd better join us. It never seems to work when I'm not at the end... What a filthy night it's turning into. I'm afraid you'll all be drenched tomorrow but of course you'll say it doesn't matter.

RAYMOND
It doesn't.

Beyond him, Isobel is listening to Anthony on her other side.

ANTHONY
What do you mean he's losing interest in that sort of thing?

ISOBEL
Not just that. The whole Empire. He thinks the steam's gone out of it.

Anxiously Anthony talks down the table, making the conversation general.

ANTHONY
That's not true is it, William? That you think the Empire's finished?

FREDDIE
Surely everyone feels the war changed things. Don't they?

LAVINIA
I don't care *what's* changed or not changed as long as our sons are spared what you all went through.

SYLVIA
Not *all*. You never fought, did you, William?

30 CONTINUED: (3)

WILLIAM
I did my bit.

LOUISA
Of course you did.

SYLVIA
Well, you made a lot of money but it's not quite the same as charging into the cannon's mouth, is it? Thank God for Raymond. At least the family had one representative in the front line.

Mabel turns to Ivor on her right, speaking sotto voce.

MABEL
What about Commander Meredith? He must have done something right.

IVOR
Not much. After ten years in the navy you're made Lieutenant Commander if you're not dead or in prison. No, Stockbridge was the hero. Once he captured an entire battalion single-handed. He wal
ked into the middle of them by accident and instead of panicking he told them he was the advance guard whereupon they all flung down their rifles on the spot. Trouble was there were three thousand of them and only one of him…

MABEL
But how *splendid!*

SYLVIA
It *was* splendid. How many times were you mentioned in despatches, Raymond?

RAYMOND
I forget.

Throughout this, George and Arthur move round the table. Jennings stands surveying his troops. He moves forward from time to time to replenish an empty (red) wine glass. He is at the table when he sees Elsie. Crossing over to her, he is almost fierce.

JENNINGS
What do you think you're doing here?

(CONTINUED)

30 CONTINUED: (4)

ELSIE
Mrs Wilson asked me to tell you that the others have come.

This does ameliorate her fault. He goes to Sylvia's right, speaking in a low voice.

JENNINGS
Lord Rupert Standish and Mr Blond have arrived, milady.

SYLVIA
No, they're too late. Give them a tray in the billiard room. They can join us later.

JENNINGS
Very good, milady.

Isobel has heard. She leans over eagerly, her plain face flushed with pleasure.

ISOBEL
Is Rupert here? Shall I go and say hello?

SYLVIA
I don't think so… Thank you, Jennings.

As Jennings walks away, we can just hear one final interchange.

MABEL
But I'm not a country girl at all.

IVOR
Oh?

MABEL
No. I grew up in Leicester. My father had a glove factory. One thing I do know is how a glove should fit.

FREDDIE
Really, darling! You're boring poor Mr Novello to *death*!

Off camera, Ivor protests "Not at all" as Jennings reaches the door.

31 INT. BILLIARD-ROOM. NIGHT.

Arthur is carrying a tray and he moves discreetly as the two young men play billiards in a pool of light from the overhead fitting. They pay the footman no attention.

JEREMY
Face it. You're a younger son. With the tastes of a marquess and the income of a vicar. Here's the solution. She likes you. Her mother likes you. She's not exactly a show-stopper but you can't have everything.

RUPERT
Why's it so important to you?

JEREMY
Because if you marry badly, who's going to give me decent shooting in my old age?

RUPERT
The father's not keen on the idea.

JEREMY
He'll come round.'Have you met my daughter, Lady Rupert Standish?'

RUPERT
Maybe... He thinks I'm after her money.

JEREMY
Of course he does but you can't let that put you off... "Faint heart never won fair lady." Or, in this case, *rich* lady.

RUPERT
He's more of an obstacle than you think.

JEREMY
Then you must overcome it, mustn't you?

During this, Arthur quietly unloads plates from a tray onto a bridge table laid with a cloth, silver and glass. He strikes a match to light the candles in its centre. The noise and flash of flame alert the young men to his presence and they straighten up.

31 CONTINUED:

ARTHUR
Her ladyship asks if you would join her in the drawing-room after you've finished.

RUPERT
Certainly.

ARTHUR
If you'd ring when you're ready for your next course…

He indicates a bell pull in the dado.

JEREMY
We will. Thank you.

Arthur goes. As he leaves Rupert speaks softly.

RUPERT
Do you think he heard?

32 INT. DINING-ROOM. NIGHT.

The men are standing as the women leave. Jennings is the only servant present.

SYLVIA
Now, don't be too long.

William shuts the door and returns to his seat, inviting the other men to join him.

WILLIAM
Move up, all of you… Thank you, Jennings.

They sit at his end of the table, irrespective of where they were before.

WEISSMAN
I don't suppose there's any sign of my telephone call?

JENNINGS
Not yet, I'm afraid, sir. The lines can be very busy…

Jennings places a decanter of port in front of William, removing its stopper.

32 CONTINUED:

JENNINGS (CONT'D)
Would you like me to ask Lord Rupert and Mr Blond to join you, sir?

WILLIAM
Leave them be. They can entertain the ladies. Give Mr Novello a rest.

FREDDIE
Is that Rupert Standish? Has he arrived?

ANTHONY
Why? Do you know him?

FREDDIE
Certainly. We younger sons have to stick together. We've a lot in common.

He imagines this will amuse William but, instead, his host looks at him with disdain as he pours himself a glass and passes the port to his left. Jennings brings the cigars.

WILLIAM
Yes. I expect you have.

The butler leaves and we go with him.

33 INT. SCULLERY. NIGHT.

Among the bottles in this ancillary room, there are two with the skull and cross bones sign of poison. Bertha checks the contents of a drawer. Mrs Croft is watching her.

BERTHA
Arthur said he had to shout it down the table. Makes you feel sorry for him.

MRS CROFT
He's got nothing to be ashamed of. It's not his fault if they put him in an orphanage.

BERTHA
It's nobody's fault if it comes to that.

MRS CROFT
How do you know?

(CONTINUED)

33 CONTINUED:

BERTHA
No. It's not here. And Mr Jennings is certain he hasn't got it?

MRS CROFT
So he says.

BERTHA
But if it's a silver carving knife, he *must* have it. It's just gone in the wrong drawer in the silver pantry. It wouldn't have been put in here.

MRS CROFT
That's what I told him… How old would you say he was?

For a moment Bertha is puzzled then she remembers what they were talking about.

BERTHA
What do you think? Thirty one or two? Why?

MRS CROFT
No reason… I think I'll turn in. We've got an early start.

34 INT. WEISSMAN BEDROOM. NIGHT.

Weissman, in his dressing-gown, reads a book by the fire in this sumptuous room.

WEISSMAN
Of course he won't mind. I'll just say I want you with me… By the way, I talked to Sheehan at the studio. The figures are worse than they thought. Not a single winner in the year. He sounded pretty desperate.

He looks at the valet.

WEISSMAN (CONT'D)
Will you come back later?

HENRY
I don't think I should risk it, do you?

There is something smug in the way he says this. He goes to the door.

(CONTINUED)

34 CONTINUED:

WEISSMAN
Oh Henry, don't forget those. Or they'll think you don't care.

Coolly, he nods at his dirty shirt, socks and underpants on a chair. They exchange a

look. Silently, Henry picks them up and leaves.

35 INT. SYLVIA'S BEDROOM. NIGHT.

Lewis helps Sylvia into a silk *peignoir*. The four-poster bed has been turned down. An embroidered, gauze blanket-cover has replaced the counterpane.

LEWIS
Pleasant evening, milady?

SYLVIA
Not really… I'm worn out.

She throws herself back among the pillows. Lewis strains to hang the frock. She is old and the effort is great. But if there is irony in their situation, neither is aware of it.

SYLVIA (CONT'D)
Is there any chocolate left in that pot?

Lewis pauses to lift the lid of an exquisite little Sèvres pot on the dressing table.

LEWIS
I'll go down and make some more.

36 INT. GALLERY. NIGHT.

Lewis vanishes through the door to the back staircase as Henry Denton enters the gallery. He is passing Sylvia's door when it suddenly flies open.

SYLVIA
Lewis!

The suddenness of her apparition startles him for a moment. He returns Sylvia's gaze.

SYLVIA (CONT'D)
I was looking for my maid.

36 CONTINUED:

HENRY
She's just gone downstairs. Can I help?

SYLVIA
She's fetching some chocolate for me but I'd rather have a glass of milk.

HENRY
Would that be hot milk? Or cold?

SYLVIA
What do you think?

HENRY
I couldn't say, milady.

SYLVIA
Hot, then... and with something to make it *sweet*...or I know I'll never shut my eyes.

HENRY
Why? Do you have trouble sleeping, milady?

SYLVIA
Well,I've a feeling I will tonight. In fact, I know I'll be wide awake at one and bored to sobs...

HENRY
Then we must try to think of something to amuse you -

As Barnes appears through a door further down, they break off, their contract made. Sylvia closes her door as Henry hears Anthony's voice.

ANTHONY (VO)
I *knew* it. I *knew* he had something like this planned –

Barnes rolls his eyes in Henry's direction as they push through onto the back stair.

37 INT. FOOTMEN'S ATTIC CORRIDOR. NIGHT.

Mary is climbing the stairs. At the top, she stops. She is clearly lost. After a moment, she goes to one of the doors and knocks. There is an invitation to 'come in.'

38 INT. ROBERT'S ATTIC ROOM. NIGHT.

Henry is in his shirtsleeves. He looks up as Mary enters. She stands, dumbstruck.

MARY
Oh… I'm ever so sorry… I must have taken the wrong stairs…

But Henry is too quick for her. He pushes the door shut behind her.

HENRY
Don't want to be seen up here or you'll be for it.

MARY
I'd better go down…

HENRY
There's no rush, is there? Since you're here now…

She is frozen, receiving his advances like a gazelle cornered by a tiger.

HENRY (CONT'D)
What about a drink? I think we've both earned one.

Out of his bag on the bed, he takes a bottle of whisky and sloshes some into two toothmugs on the wash stand. Holding out the glass with one hand, he slips the other round her waist, pulls her to him and leans to kiss her when, she is suddenly transformed into a vicious, spitting, fighting cat. As he backs away, stunned, they hear the noise of someone on the stairs. Quick as a flash, Mary pulls herself together. When the door opens and Robert enters, there is no trace left of the rumpus. Naturally, he is amazed to see her.

ROBERT
What's this? Why are you in here?

MARY
I came up the wrong staircase…I was just waiting 'til the coast was clear.

ROBERT
Well, you'd better get down again. Before anyone catches you.

(CONTINUED)

Holding open the door, he checks the corridor and nods. She goes. He shuts the door.

ROBERT (CONT'D)
I think she's nice, that one.

HENRY
Then you'd better go after her. You know what they say. He who hesitates is lost.

This is not Robert's style at all but, if anything, he is amused by his companion's brashness. Henry scoops up the fallen mug and smoothly pours two more drinks.

HENRY (CONT'D)
So what do you make of the place?

Robert shrugs. He sips the drink and sits, watching Henry hang his things.

HENRY (CONT'D)
I mean, is this a well run house, would you say? Do you think Sir William would be good to work for?

ROBERT
No.

He does not elaborate. After a moment, Henry continues.

HENRY
How long have you been doing this?

ROBERT
What? Valeting? About seven years. I was a footman before that.

HENRY
And working for Lord Stockbridge. Is that a promotion?

ROBERT
No. I used to be with the Earl of Flintshire.

HENRY
Then why did you move?

ROBERT
'Cos I felt like it.

Henry nods. Beside Robert's bed there is a framed but old photograph of a woman.

HENRY
Who's that?

ROBERT
My mum.

HENRY
Where's she live?

ROBERT
She doesn't. That's why they put me in the orphanage.

HENRY
Of course. I'm sorry… What happened to her?

ROBERT
What d'you mean?

HENRY
Well… why did she die. I mean, was she young? Was it in childbirth?

ROBERT
You're not very curious, are you? Yes, she was young. She worked in a factory, she had me and a little while later she died. End of story.

HENRY
So why didn't you say she was a factory worker at dinner?

ROBERT
'Cos I didn't fancy discussing my private life with a table of strangers.

He picks up a book. Even Henry is aware that he has overstepped the mark.

HENRY
I'm sorry if I spoke out of turn, mate. Didn't mean to offend you.

ROBERT
I'm not offended. And don't call me 'mate.'

(CONTINUED)

38 CONTINUED: (3)

He returns his attention to his book. During this last exchange, Henry has put his jacket and tie back on again. He looks down at Robert. Clearly he is not going to get any more out of him.

HENRY
Well. See you later. I've got a date with a glass of milk.

He slips out of the room.

39 INT. ELSIE'S ATTIC ROOM. NIGHT.

Elsie pulls off her cap and shoes and slips out of her dress. Mary is finishing unpacking. She is still a little shaken. Elsie flops onto the bed.

ELSIE
Shouldn't worry about it. Goes with the territory… I'm bushed. I think Mrs Wilson forgets I do Miss Isobel on top of everything else.

She is flicking through a Hollywood fan magazine. "Watch Your Step, Ann Dvorak!" or "Joan Crawford and Douglas Fairbanks: Of Course It's For Keeps!" Until…

ELSIE (CONT'D)
Ooh, look.

There is a still of Ivor Novello with Benita Hume. Mary looks over her shoulder.

MARY
Just think of him sleeping downstairs…

ELSIE
I shall have to watch you, my girl. I can see that.

MARY
Her ladyship says that Mr Weissman's a Hollywood producer. He makes the Charlie Chan films.

ELSIE
I like those. I enjoy a bit of a fright in the cinema.

MARY
You could go with his valet. He'd give you a fright.

They laugh together. Mary wrinkles her nose.

MARY (CONT'D)
You'd better keep your eye on him… I think he's a funny one. He's not from Scotland for a start. At least not from any part of it that *I* know.

Elsie shrugs and goes back to her magazine.

MARY (CONT'D)
What's Mrs Nesbitt like?

ELSIE
She's O.K. I feel a bit sorry for her, really… 'Course it never works.

MARY
What never works?

ELSIE
When a man like that marries beneath him. He hasn't got the brains to carry it off.

MARY
I think it's romantic. To marry for love.

Mary picks up Elsie's dress and cap. Elsie is more interested in her magazine.

ELSIE
Oh, it wasn't love. Not him. He's a nasty piece of work. The 'honourable' Freddie Nesbitt. That's a laugh. It was her father's money he was after but there was less than he thought. Now it's spent and all he's got to show is a wife he's ashamed of. *And* he's lost his job. He wants Miss Isobel to put in a word with Sir William.

MARY
Will she?

ELSIE
She might.

MARY
Why should she?

39 CONTINUED: (2)

ELSIE
Well, listen to you. Miss Nosie Parker… What's the matter?

Mary has been distracted by the sight of a crumpled shirt on the chest.

MARY
I never washed that shirt. That's me in trouble...unless I do it now...

ELSIE
Do you want me to come with you?

MARY
No, no. You stay there. I'll be all right.

40 INT. STILL ROOM. NIGHT.

Mary pulls the plug from the sink and wrings out the shirt. Then leaves the room, crossing the corridor on her way to the ironing room.

41 OMITTED

42 OMITTED

42A INT. IRONING AND SEWING ROOM. NIGHT.

Mary enters the dark room, turning on the light. There is a scuffling sound.

MARY
Is someone there?

There is silence. Then a smothered giggle.

MARY (CONT'D)
Come on. Who is it? You're scaring me.

Shyly, Bertha emerges from the shadows, smoothing down her skirts.

MARY (CONT'D)
What are you up to?

She speaks as she lowers the drying rack over the stove, arranges the shirt on it and winds it up again. Bertha shrugs.

BERTHA
Nothing.

(CONTINUED)

42A CONTINUED:

She's not giving anything away. Mary nods and moves off but as she is about to leave the room, she looks back into the dark corner where a shaft of moonlight illuminates black shoes, crumpled trousers and underpants revealing the hairy lower calves of a man. The rest of him is in shadow. He is quite still. Without a word, she hurries out.

43 INT. KITCHEN CORRIDOR. NIGHT.

Mary is walking down the corridor when Mrs Wilson emerges.

MRS WILSON
Miss Trentham? Can I help you?

MARY
I was just washing a shirt of her ladyship's.

MRS WILSON
I hope you found everything you needed. Lady Trentham's tea will be laid out in the still-room any time after seven tomorrow. We've remembered the cucumbers. Her breakfast tray may be collected at a quarter to nine.

MARY
She likes it at half past eight.

MRS WILSON
I know but the shooting breakfast can delay the trays a little. It won't be later. They move off at nine. Does she have to have marmalade? Dorothy made too little last January so we've run out of our own... She wouldn't care for strawberry jam, I suppose?

MARY
Not really...

MRS WILSON
Very well. It isn't a problem.

There is a noise. Sir William McCordle is approaching down the corridor.

43 CONTINUED:

WILLIAM
Oh... I was rather hoping for a word with Mrs Wilson.

MARY
Of course, sir.

WILLIAM
Mrs Wilson, I wonder if you could tell Jennings that I want the soup after the fourth drive tomorrow…

Is this really what he came to say? As Mary goes, Mrs Wilson has closed the door.

44 INT. FOOTMEN'S ATTIC CORRIDOR. NIGHT.

Henry backs out of the bedroom door, shuts it carefully, and sets off down the stairs.

45 EXT. GOSFORD PARK. DAY.

It is a grey morning. Men gather as two wagonettes are pulled up to the front.

46 INT. TRENTHAM BEDROOM. DAY.

A fire crackles merrily in the grate. Constance is sitting up in bed. She smooths the sheet before her, eagerly anticipating the tray that Mary is carrying in from the door.

CONSTANCE
They always send up a good breakfast here. I'll say that for Sylvia. She's not at all mean in *that* way…

Mary places the pretty tray across her mistress. Constance lifts the lid of a china jam pot and wrinkles her nose.

CONSTANCE (CONT'D)
*Bought marmalade*! Dear me. I call that very feeble… Oh well. I suppose one can't have everything. Mary, I don't think I *will* wear that shirt after all. The check's warmer and that's all I care about.

She starts to eat. Mary, suppressing irritation, looks out of the window.

46 CONTINUED:

MARY
They're just getting ready to move off.

CONSTANCE
Ugh. Look. It's already starting to rain.

MARY
You'll enjoy the luncheon.

CONSTANCE
Nursery stew in a howling draft? I doubt it.

47 EXT. GOSFORD PARK. DAY.

Strutt is with the loaders. It is drizzling slightly.

STRUTT
We're only six guns now and, apart from Sir William, they're shooting doubles or singles so we won't need you all. D'you want to toss for it?

DERWENT
What happened?

STRUTT
The American gentleman. He's a vegetarian. And vegetarians don't shoot, apparently.

CROSBIE
Bloody hell...

They all start to laugh, including Strutt, but then he quietens them down.

STRUTT
That'll do. And remember, no comments on the skills of the gun you're loading for unless you're asked. Understood? That goes for you too, Baker.

BAKER
Honestly, Mr Strutt. I thought he had asked...

(CONTINUED)

47 CONTINUED:

STRUTT
Well, he thought he hadn't. And straight faces. Even if they can't hit a barn door.

48 INT. SERVANTS' HALL. DAY.

Henry, in his overcoat, is being interrogated by Barnes, Robert, George and Arthur. Probert is polishing a fob watch and a couple of the maids, including Mary, look on.

BARNES
What d'you mean you're *'going shooting'*?

HENRY
Mr Weissman wants me to accompany him. Nothing wrong in that.

ARTHUR
But what for? You're not even loading. He hasn't got a gun.

HENRY
Well… he might need something.

GEORGE
What could he need?

George is imitating Henry's voice insultingly. Probert comes to Henry's aid.

PROBERT
Of course the very idea of service is offensive to you, George, but there's no need to take it out on the rest of us. Please forgive our ill manners, Mr Weissman.

Henry smiles a trifle nervously as he heads for the door.

BARNES
I think he's got something to hide, that one.

PROBERT
We've all got something to hide, Mr Meredith.

Robert catches Mary's eye as he picks up a newspaper from the table.

49 EXT. GOSFORD PARK. DAY.

Henry, out of place in his coat, slips from a side door looking around for Weissman.

BAKER
Who's that?

STRUTT
Haven't a clue. Right. Baker, you take Lord Stockbridge. You won't have to teach him much. Derwent and Crosbie, Sir William as usual. Tozer, Mr Nesbitt there…

Once instructed, the men break away from the group and approach the gun they have been allotted to. William has three guns shared between his two loaders. Stockbridge, Standish and Meredith all have a pair. Nesbitt and Blond have one each. William holds out a slotted pouch containing flat, ivory spills. One by one, the guns choose a spill and read a number although William keeps his finger fixed on one. At the end, he pulls it out before gathering the others.

WILLIAM
I'm Four. Right. We're turning on six. Evens go up two, odds down two. No ground game. Any white pheasants will cost you a fiver.

WEISSMAN
I'll come and cheer you on.

But this suggestion does not seem to find favour. As Weissman settles himself into the wagonette, Raymond, next to him, speaks softly.

RAYMOND
He won't let you. He can't stand witnesses.

WEISSMAN
But I keep hearing how he's such an expert.

RAYMOND
He's an expert gunsmith. It isn't quite the same as being a good shot…

WEISSMAN
Why wouldn't he let anyone have number four?

(CONTINUED)

49 CONTINUED:

RAYMOND
Why do you think? It's the best peg… That fellow's trying to attract your attention.

Weissman looks over to where the oddly-dressed Henry stands and beckons him over.

WEISSMAN
It's just my man… It's all right for him to keep me company, isn't it?

Raymond looks at him. Clearly this is an amazing suggestion.

50 INT. ISOBEL'S BEDROOM. DAY.

Isobel gazes out at the garden.

ELSIE
Do you want to change now, miss? Or shall I come back later?

ISOBEL
He won't do it.

ELSIE
Who won't do what, miss?

ISOBEL
My father… He won't give Freddie a job. I spoke to him last night and he said he'd think about it but this morning, he says it isn't up to him – when of course it is…

ELSIE
Why not?

ISOBEL
I don't know. Something to do with why Freddie was sacked but I can't get a straight answer out of either of them…

ELSIE
Well, you've done your best. Mr Nesbitt can't ask more than that.

ISOBEL
Oh, but he can. *Much* more… He says he's going to tell him.

(CONTINUED)

50 CONTINUED:

She has risen to her feet and is roaming the room like an animal. This is a facer.

ELSIE
Do you think he will?

ISOBEL
I don't know... He says Daddy'll give him a job to keep him quiet.

She hesitates. She turns back to Elsie, her awkward face vivid with desperation.

ISOBEL (CONT'D)
Could you say something?

ELSIE
To Mr Nesbitt?

ISOBEL
To Daddy.

ELSIE
Really, miss. Why ever would you think I could make any difference?

Her tone is disingenuous but Isobel looks at her coolly.

ISOBEL
Will you?

51 EXT. AN OPEN DRIVE. DAY.

The drive is about to begin. A horn blows. McCordle is ready, gun in hand. Behind him stand his loaders, Derwent and Crosbie, each holding a gun. The first flush of birds fly over. Sir William lifts his gun and fires both barrels, one after the other.

WILLIAM
Damn!

He swiftly changes guns with Derwent who reloads as Sir William fires again.

WILLIAM (CONT'D)
Blast!

He changes guns with Crosbie who starts to reload. More shots from Sir William.

51 CONTINUED:

WILLIAM (CONT'D)
I think I pricked that one.

From the expressions of the loaders as they share a look, it is clear they do not agree. The shooting is heavy now until suddenly a shot just misses them. All three duck.

DERWENT
Bugger me!

CROSBIE
You all right, sir?

WILLIAM
No. I am *not* all right.

To his and their astonishment, a tiny trickle of blood marks his ear.

CROSBIE
Blimey.

WILLIAM
Where the bloody hell did that come from?

DERWENT
Further down the line, sir.

WILLIAM
At the end of the drive, find Strutt. See if he knows. If he does, he can tell the gun responsible to go back to the house.

CROSBIE
Here they come again, sir.

WILLIAM
Right.

With a sigh of recovery, he takes up his gun again and fires.

WILLIAM (CONT'D)
Damn it!

Crosbie looks over to Derwent and rolls his eyes skyward.

52 INT. TRENTHAM BEDROOM. DAY.

Mary comes in. Constance is at the dressing-table. Sylvia lies on the bed. Louisa and Lavinia are seated.

(CONTINUED)

52 CONTINUED:

They are all dressed for a shooting lunch in rather heartier tweeds than they travelled in. They wear walking shoes and are already in country hats.

CONSTANCE
Did you find one?

MARY
Oh yes.

She kneels down by her mistress and takes out a brown shoelace. With Constance's foot on her lap, Mary removes the broken one and replaces it during the scene.

LAVINIA
Well?

SYLVIA
There's no point in looking at me. If I open my mouth on the subject, it'll only make things worse.

LOUISA
I've already tried. I don't mind having another go but it won't do any good.

The door opens and Isobel appears. She is now in her tweeds which are not becoming. The others whisper conspiratorially. 'Come in!' or 'Shut the door!'

ISOBEL
Jennings says the cars are ready.

CONSTANCE
Goody. I'm starving. I do *love* a shooting luncheon.

Mary looks up. Sylvia is examining her daughter dispassionately.

SYLVIA
What *are* you wearing?

ISOBEL
Why? Don't you like it? You bought it.

SYLVIA
Did I? How extraordinary of me… Come on. We'd better get going. Where's the wretched Mabel? Is she downstairs?

(CONTINUED)

52 CONTINUED: (2)

CONSTANCE
And has anyone checked her outfit? She's probably in black velvet with a feather in her hair.

LAVINIA
She's in the morning-room looking perfectly normal. And don't be such a snob, Aunt Constance.

CONSTANCE
Me? I haven't a snobbish bone in my body.

She goes, indignant at the charge. Isobel at the rear, shares this moment with Mary.

53 INT. ROBERT'S ATTIC ROOM. DAY.

MRS WILSON
I'm sorry, I didn't realise you were in - just my routine inspection.

ROBERT
What can I do for you?

MRS WILSON
I'm sorry? So how are you settling in with Lord Stockbridge? I know you haven't been with him for long. You know smoking isn't allowed up here.

Stubs cigarette - sees photo.

MRS WILSON (CONT'D)
I hope you have everything you require to make his Lordship comfortable. We haven't forgotten anything.

ROBERT
I can't believe you forget much Mrs Wilson.

54 EXT./INT. OPEN FIELD/TEMPLE. DAY.

George is in the back of a farm truck with large baskets surrounding him. There are also crates of wine, jugs and bowls of various sizes, covered with white cloths.

(CONTINUED)

54 CONTINUED:

The vehicle approaches a temple with a terrace on which we can see that the guns, Ivor, Weissman and the ladies have gathered. Below it, Jennings is running forward.

JENNINGS
Where have you been? They've already broken for luncheon. Take the Bloody Mary. And hurry.

George lifts two covered jugs from a bucket of ice on the floor of the wagon and starts toward the temple. He passes McCordle and Strutt. The latter is shaking his head.

STRUTT
Well, they didn't, sir. It was a heavy drive, the loaders were busy and nobody saw. I'm sorry.

George, carrying his jugs, takes the camera over to the bottom of a stone staircase where Raymond and Sylvia stand. As usual, we hear only what the footman hears.

RAYMOND
I'm warning you.

SYLVIA
What? What *exactly* are you warning me of?

She falls silent as she sees the footman. At the top of the stair, George enters the temple. Jennings hurries in behind him and starts to unload the stew from the baskets. Henry Denton watches as George arranges glasses on a tray.

HENRY
Can I do anything to help, Mr Jennings?

Jennings is threatened with the spectre of bad management. After a second, he nods.

JENNINGS
Well, since you're here… you might take the sherry round…

Henry lifts a tray with a decanter and glasses. As he and George start for the terrace, they pass the Merediths who appear to be arguing out of sight of the other guests.

LAVINIA
Just calm down.

54 CONTINUED: (2)

ANTHONY
You don't seem to understand how serious this is.

LAVINIA
We'll manage, we always have.

ANTHONY
Oh yes. And how long do you think we'll go on managing if he sticks to it. I don't see why you can't get your sisters to help.

LAVINIA
Darling, I've tried. Of course I've tried. But you know what they're like.

ANTHONY
I know they couldn't care less if we go under. Why should they? Their dressmakers will still be busy and their dinners served on time.

LAVINIA
What does that matter? Why can't you see that we've got what they'll never have. And they know it. Do you honestly think I'd change places with either of them?

ANTHONY
That's not the point.

LAVINIA
Isn't it? Anyway, promise me you'll leave it for now. This is *not* the right moment.

ANTHONY
There is no sodding right moment!

Anthony moves outside. McCordle is talking to Jeremy and Rupert. Anthony waits for him as George and Henry start to hand round the drinks. We follow them and hear snatches of what is being said. All these exchanges overlap each other.

FREDDIE
That's your problem.

ISOBEL
But I don't see what more I can do.

54 CONTINUED: (3)

In the background, Sylvia is winding a gramophone. She lifts the needle and it starts to play "The Land Of Might Have Been." A few clap as Ivor bows to his hostess.

IVOR
Very tactful.

SYLVIA
I thought so. I borrowed it off Lewis.

CONSTANCE
Isn't this fun? There's nothing like a day out with the guns, is there?

SYLVIA
Nothing. Shall we go in? It's going to pelt in a minute.

Ivor moves over to Weissman taking a telegram out of his pocket.

IVOR
I nearly forgot. This came for you. About an hour ago.

Henry joins them as Weissman reads it.

HENRY
Good or bad?

WEISSMAN
Neither. Winfield Sheehan wants to talk to me. I'll call him later.

He explains to Ivor.

WEISSMAN (CONT'D)
The Head of Production at Fox. He's handling the next Charlie Chan.

Isobel has left Freddie and joins Rupert, passing Jeremy and Raymond on the way.

JEREMY
You had a fantastic one in the third drive. It was a mile high.

RAYMOND
That's generous but I don't think so.

RUPERT
Would you like to come and see how we manage it at Stanton?
(MORE)

54 CONTINUED: (4)

RUPERT (CONT'D)
Next month perhaps. I can give you four dates to choose from.

This is to Isobel who smiles. Then she sees as Jeremy winks at Rupert. Behind, McCordle crosses. Anthony pounces.

ANTHONY
William!

He tries what he imagines is a casual chuckle.

ANTHONY (CONT'D)
You weren't serious last night, were you?

WILLIAM
I'm afraid so. I was going to tell you next week but since you asked...

William is irritated. This is exactly what he wanted to avoid. He looks about for help and seeing George, he holds up his glass for some more.

ANTHONY
The thing is... I don't think you've grasped what this would do to the whole project. What it would do to me.

WILLIAM
Come on. It's not as black as all that.

ANTHONY
Yes, it bloody well is.

WILLIAM
Well, I'm sorry to hear it, Anthony. But business is business. I'm not a Charity Commissioner, you know.

ANTHONY
For Christ's sake, William, I'm begging you –

Impulsively, he siezes the other man's forearm forgetting about the full glass of Bloody Mary. It shatters on the paving. Anthony is horrified. He takes out a handkerchief, offering it to McCordle.

ANTHONY (CONT'D)
I'm so sorry, old man...

54 CONTINUED: (5)

WILLIAM
Just leave it.

His anger is obvious but contained as George stoops to pick up the pieces and Jennings comes into the doorway. He is just in time. The rain is starting again.

JENNINGS
Luncheon is served.

The company hurries in to the gorgeous table where the servants wait for them.

CONSTANCE
I love a picnic, don't you?

55 INT. MAIDS' ATTIC CORRIDOR. DAY.

Elsie, in a dressing-gown and carrying a sponge bag, opens a door at the end of the corridor. We hear a squawk and a splash.

56 INT. SERVANTS' ATTIC BATHROOM. DAY.

The room is small and spartan without decoration of any sort. Mary, embarrassed and covering herself, has been surprised in the bath.

MARY
Shut the door for heaven's sake.

ELSIE
It's only Lewis. If any of the men were found up here they'd be sacked on the spot. Worse luck.

She settles herself on the mean, cork-covered stool. Mary finishes her washing, uneasily concealed behind her arm and her flannel. Elsie watches her, amused

ELSIE (CONT'D)
Don't tell me you're a convent girl. Or is it Presbyterian modesty? Is the water hot?

MARY
Not very.

ELSIE
No. And it won't be 'til the guns come home. I'd better get into yours.

56 CONTINUED:

MARY
Her Ladyship says Sir William loves his shooting.

ELSIE
Yeah, he does. Can't hit a barn door but he does love it. Sweet, really.

MARY
Last night - no, I shouldn't say.

ELSIE
Yes, you should. What is it?

MARY
Only that...when I went down to wash that shirt, I think he was in the ironing-room. With one of the kitchen maids.

ELSIE
No. It wouldn't have been him.

She is surprisingly definite.

MARY
I think it was. Leastways, he came down the passage a moment later and I don't see how -

ELSIE
No, it wasn't him. Hurry up.

She starts to undress.

56A INT. SERVANTS ATTIC BATHROOM. DAY

Now Mary is putting on her dressing-gown and drying her hair while Elsie is in the bath. She is more comfortable to bathe with a witness than Mary was. They have settled into a gossip.

MARY
You know when you said Sir William could have had his pick? Between Lady Sylvia and Lady Stockbridge?

ELSIE
Yes.

56A CONTINUED:

MARY
Well, I asked her Ladyship about it and she said...they cut cards for him.

She shares the wicked thought with Elsie.

ELSIE
No!

MARY
I can't believe it either. I s'pose it was a joke.

ELSIE
I wouldn't be too sure. I heard...

She breaks off with a sigh, catching herself out.

ELSIE (CONT'D)
Just listen to me.

MARY
What?

ELSIE
Why do we spend our time living through them...? Look at poor old Lewis. If her own mother had a heart attack, she'd think it was less important than one of Lady Sylvia's farts. He always says -

She remembers herself and breaks off.

MARY
Who? Who says what?

ELSIE
Never mind. Doesn't matter...I dunno...all I want is to be at the centre of my own life. 'Course if you say that in this house, Mr Jennings thinks you're planning to blow up the Romanovs.

There is a bang on the door. From outside we hear an anguished voice.

LEWIS
Are you ever coming out?

57 INT. TRENTHAM BEDROOM. EVE.

Mary is fastening Constance into another of the dresses that we saw being hung up earlier with another of the sets of jewels. The mistress is in a jolly mood.

CONSTANCE
You *must* know. You can't fool me. If there's one thing I *don't* look for in a maid, it's discretion. Except with my own secrets, of course.

MARY
Well, I don't know much, milady… Apparently, he was counting on Sir William for an investment and had "guaranteed his interest" – whatever that means… Anyway, Mr Barnes – the Commander's valet – said he wanted to leave at once but Lady Lavinia's persuaded him to stay until tomorrow. To make less of a thing of it.

There is a brisk knock and Sylvia enters. She completely ignores Mary.

SYLVIA
I'm on my way down. This is just a quick warning. For God's sake be careful not to rub him up, tonight.

CONSTANCE
I don't know what you mean.

SYLVIA
You know exactly what I mean. He's in a filthy mood. With everyone… He's talking about stopping your allowance.

CONSTANCE
But it's for life! That was settled! He can't do that!

SYLVIA
Just you watch him. He's absolutely spoiling for a fight and if you'll take my advice, you won't give him one… I've got to go.

She hurries out. This exchange has been in and out of vision as we follow Mary putting things away. Constance catches her eye through the mirror.

(CONTINUED)

57 CONTINUED:

CONSTANCE
Now that you *can* be discreet about…

58 INT. UPSTAIRS HALL AND CORRIDOR. EVE.

Jennings, with whisky, glasses etc., crosses the hall. Weissman is on the telephone.

WEISSMAN
What am I going to do about it? I'm going to call his Goddamn bluff. I'll meet his fucking deadline. That's what I'm going to do about it!

We just see Sylvia and Louisa respond to his language as Jennings gets to the library.

59 INT. LIBRARY. EVE.

Jennings opens the door without knocking. He stops dead. Three men are seated round the fire. William, Novello and *Henry*. William is surly as he pets his dog.

WILLIAM
Is her ladyship down yet?

JENNINGS
They're just assembling in the drawing-room now, sir.

WILLIAM
Well, it won't kill them to wait five minutes.

He starts to pour as Weissman comes in behind him, taking a drink from the tray.

WEISSMAN
Wait for it: Sheehan wants a final script by the fifteenth.

IVOR
That's crazy. You've only just worked out the story.

WILLIAM
That's all, Jennings.

WEISSMAN (VO)
He knows that. He's just wants an excuse to renegotiate.
(MORE)

(CONTINUED)

59 CONTINUED:

WEISSMAN (VO) (CONT'D)
He thinks he's losing the studio...
There's talk about Zanuck coming in...

But during this Jennings has left and we with him.

60 INT. KITCHEN CORRIDOR. EVE.

Jennings is walking toward his own room when Mrs Croft sees him.

MRS CROFT
Oh, Mr Jennings, has that knife turned
up yet?

JENNINGS
Not now.

He goes into his room and shuts the door. Further down the corridor, Mrs Wilson is watching. Mrs Croft retrieves her dignity and retreats into the kitchen.

61 INT. DINING-ROOM. EVE.

Dinner is almost finished. In contrast to the night before, the atmosphere is terrible. George, Arthur and Elsie are carrying round the savouries. Jennings pours wine. William is sulking. A few of the guests are trying to keep things going.

LAVINIA
Goodness, isn't it pretty, here? The
house has such a lovely position.

RAYMOND
The best view's from the old water
tower. We might walk up there
tomorrow. I suppose you really do have
to get back to London?

ANTHONY
I'm afraid we should. When you're
ruined, there's such a lot to do.

This succeeds in further flattening the company as well as exasperating Lavinia and infuriating William. The servants exchange glances as they labour on round.

CONSTANCE
Would anyone care for a game of bridge
after dinner?

FREDDIE
I wouldn't mind.

(CONTINUED)

CONSTANCE
Who else? What about you, Louisa?

LOUISA
I don't think so. I've rather gone off cards. I've never been very lucky with them.

Almost inadvertently, she catches William's eye. He holds her glance, subdued.

WILLIAM
Nor me.

For some reason, this both annoys Sylvia and spurs her into her duty as a hostess.

SYLVIA
Tell me again, Mr Weissman, what's this film you're working on?

WEISSMAN
"Charlie Chan in London." It's a detective mystery.

MABEL
Set in London.

WEISSMAN
Not really. Most of it takes place at a country house-party. Rather like this one... That's where the murder happens.

CONSTANCE
How horrid! And who turns out to have done it?

WEISSMAN
I couldn't tell you that. It'd spoil it for you.

CONSTANCE
But none of us will ever see it.

Her rudeness is quite unconscious. Rupert feels sorry for Weissman.

RUPERT
And are you thinking of making it here?

WEISSMAN
Oh no. We'll build it in the studio. I just wanted to experience a little country living while I was in England and Ivor was good enough to say he could fix it for me.

IVOR
It was William who could fix it.

JEREMY
Are you interested in films, sir?

SYLVIA
Not likely.

WILLIAM
Why shouldn't I be? You don't know what I'm interested in.

SYLVIA
Well, I know you're interested in money and in fiddling with those dreary guns but I agree. When it comes to anything else, I'm stumped.

ELSIE
That's not fair, is it, Bill? You always –

With these words, she has broken the basic rule of domestic service. She has released terrible reverberations by speaking as she did to William. Not only has she called him 'Bill,' *she has engaged in the conversation of the family*. The table is as silent as the dead, forks are stilled in mid-air, glasses half-way to lips. Elsie realises that in one tiny second, in less than a second, she has terminated her employment in that house. After a moment of total immobility, William throws down his napkin and storms out.

Raymond is the first to break the silence. With his voice, normality returns.

RAYMOND
Sylvia, did you ever manage to track down that magnolia you were after? Because, if not, I may have rather a good substitute…

62 INT. MAIDS' ATTIC CORRIDOR. EVE.

Mary comes out of her room, heading for the stairs when Elsie, in tears, pushes past.

MARY
Elsie? What's the matter?

But the girl only goes into the room and slams the door.

63 INT. DINING-ROOM. EVE.

Mary slips in. George and Arthur, with butler's trays, are clearing. George, in baize gloves, helps himself to the end of the odd wine glass. Lingering in the room are Probert, Barnes, Sarah, Renee, Robert, Dorothy, Lewis and May.

MARY
It's true then?

GEORGE
You should have seen it.

RENEE
What's going to happen to her?

LEWIS
She'll be lucky if they don't boot her out before the morning.

MARY
But she's worked here so long…

BARNES
Shall I tell you what that means to *them*? Bugger all.

PROBERT
*Please*, Mr Meredith. There are ladies present… Where is he now?

GEORGE
In the library and he won't come out again tonight.

At this point the door opens and Jennings appears. He looks around at the company.

JENNINGS
May I ask what is going on?

63 CONTINUED:

PROBERT
We were just...

JENNINGS
George, will you join me in the drawing-room, please? May, stay and help with the clearing. The rest of you can go back downstairs. I must say I'm surprised at you.

DOROTHY
But Mr Jennings –

To her dismay, he simply turns and leaves. George winks at Mary as he follows.

GEORGE
Bet you're glad you came.

64 INT. DRAWING-ROOM. EVE.

Janet has brought in a tray. She goes into the dining room as George takes the tray to hand round the coffee. Constance is at the bridge table waiting. Rupert is talking softly to Isobel. Sylvia approaches Ivor by the chimneypiece.

SYLVIA
Ivor, darling, is it too awful to ask you to play something? And brighten things up a bit? It would be *such* a treat...

IVOR
Of course.

He and Weissman walk towards the piano.

WEISSMAN
I've booked a passage and I'll live on the 'phone 'til I sail. But I have to get back to London tomorrow. I can go by train, if you'd rather stay.

IVOR
No, no. I'll take you.

WEISSMAN
You're providing a lot of entertainment for nothing.

64 CONTINUED:

IVOR
Morris. I'm used to it.

He starts to play "The Land of Might Have Been". Rupert and Isobel go to take their places at the card table. Jeremy whispers to Rupert.

JEREMY
Good work, old chap. You're doing awfully well.

RUPERT
You don't understand. I -

George holds the tray for Constance who looks up as she pours herself a cup at Mabel lingering for a moment by the card table behind Freddie.

CONSTANCE
My maid was saying how sensible you are to travel light. After all, why *should* one wear a different frock every evening. We're not in a fashion parade.

The players have drawn for dealer and Constance has won. As Isobel cuts the cards for her, Mabel wanders over to the piano in her humiliation.

65 INT. UPSTAIRS HALL AND CORRIDOR. EVE.

Robert and Mary are walking towards one of the two green baize doors.

ROBERT
How could she let him *touch* her?

MARY
You sound as if you don't like him.

ROBERT
You'd be surprised.

MARY
All right then. Surprise me.

ROBERT
Maybe I will.

But she is distracted. From the drawing-room comes the sound of music.

(CONTINUED)

65 CONTINUED:

MARY
Listen.

66 INT. DRAWING-ROOM. EVE.

Ivor is singing another song. The players are bidding. Constance is already bored with the music.

CONSTANCE
What a lovely, long repertoire.

Rupert whispers to Isobel over their cards.

RUPERT
I was wondering if we could have a word later.

ISOBEL
Of course. If you like...

Nearby, Jeremy winks in approval, which Isobel notices. As Constance has won the bidding, Freddie is dummy. Having laid out his cards, he stands.

FREDDIE
I won't be a minute.

He walks to the door. Mabel, by the piano, watches him go.

67 INT. UPSTAIRS HALL AND CORRIDOR. EVE.

Mrs Wilson appears with a tray of coffee things. She crosses the hall.

68 INT. LIBRARY. EVE.

William works at his gun table. The tools of his hobby surround him. He has re-routed his rage and now he files a metal part with angry passion and finesse. The door opens.

WILLIAM
What do you want?

MRS WILSON
I've brought you some coffee.

WILLIAM
If I'd wanted coffee I'd have rung for it!

With an impatient gesture he knocks the tray out of her hand. She starts to pick it up.

(CONTINUED)

68 CONTINUED:

WILLIAM (CONT'D)
Never mind that! Just get me some whisky!

Silently, she stands with the tray and goes to pour the drink. Her back is to him and she takes her time. He ignores her as she sets the drink before him and leaves.

69 INT. DRAWING-ROOM. EVE.

Ivor is still singing. The house-party has had enough. Rupert is dealing the next hand.

CONSTANCE
You're spoiling us, Mr Novello. *Quel embarras de richesses*...Where on earth has Freddie got to?

JEREMY
I'll play if you like. Until he gets back.

He sits between the lovers. At the other end of the room, Anthony silently steals from the room. Lavinia starts towards him.

LAVINIA
Anthony -

But he has gone. She returns to her seat on the sofa. Meanwhile, Jennings, near the door, is in heaven. George tips the remainder of the milk jug into a cup. He then turns to the enraptured butler and whispers to him.

GEORGE
Better get some more milk, Mr Jennings… I won't be a moment.

He holds the empty jug for Jennings to see. He goes to the dining-room door.

70 INT. DINING-ROOM. EVE.

As he comes in, Janet and May have paused in their clearing. Arthur stands unashamedly by the connecting door. George almost bumps into him.

ARTHUR
Why ever have you come out?

(CONTINUED)

70 CONTINUED:

GEORGE
You can have enough of a good thing... I want a fag.

He goes.

71 INT. UPSTAIRS HALL AND CORRIDOR. EVE.

Renee, Barnes, Sarah and Probert and a reluctant Lewis creep out of the green baize door. Sarah looks back down the stairs.

SARAH
Where's Mr Denton?

The others 'sssh' her, further emphasising the illicitness of their presence.

LEWIS
This isn't right, Mr Probert.

PROBERT
Oh, go on. We're not the only ones.

He nods towards Mary standing listening a little way off. She smiles guiltily.

MARY
I couldn't resist. I was just saying to Mr Par -

She looks round and to her surprise, he has gone.

MARY (CONT'D)
Oh. He's gone.

72 INT. THE BASE OF THE KITCHEN STAIRS. EVE.

Mrs Croft, the kitchen maids and Dorothy listen. Mrs Wilson comes downstairs.

MRS WILSON
What's going on? Dorothy. Get on with your work.

MRS CROFT
Excuse me, but Dorothy is under *my* jurisdiction as well, you know. And *i* say she can listen to a spot of music if she likes.

Without another word, Mrs Wilson goes into her own room.

73 INT. MAIDS' ATTIC CORRIDOR. EVE./NIGHT.

Henry arrives at a door and knocks gently. Elsie opens it. She has been crying but she is calm now.

ELSIE
Yes? What do you want?

HENRY
I thought you might need cheering up...

ELSIE
Did you? Well, you were wrong.

She shuts the door, leaving him alone.

74 INT./EXT. BACK DOOR/COURTYARD. NIGHT.

The door opens and a pair of male legs and feet, clad in black trousers and shoes appear (it could be any of the men, above or below stairs). It is raining and, for a second, the feet hesitate. Their owner appears to spy some large, muddy walking over-shoes left by a gardener in the porch. The man slips his feet, still in their black pumps, into them. There is a noise. He freezes. Mrs Croft appears through the crack of the open door. She pulls it to and we hear the bolt. After a moment the legs approach. They strain but the door won't budge.

75 INT. DRAWING-ROOM. NIGHT.

Constance, bored to sobs, looks around as she takes a liqueur from Jennings.

CONSTANCE
Where's Anthony? You don't suppose he's gone to worry William again, do you?

SYLVIA
Even Anthony couldn't be that stupid.

Mabel looks over sharply at Constance who greets her with a cheery smile.

76 INT. UPSTAIRS HALL AND CORRIDOR. NIGHT.

The boots enter the front door, leaving a muddy trail. The music is quite audible.

77 INT. LIBRARY. NIGHT.

A secret door in the bookshelves opens gently as the booted feet slip in. Leaving a trail of mud, he moves softly across the floor until William's feet come into view. The camera moves up to reveal William in a fiercely concentrated position, holding some part of a gun quite still. He seems frozen. The empty glass is on its side on the table. The hand of the intruder lifts into sight. It is covered in a green baize glove, the type we have seen in Scenes 15 and 61 and it holds the missing knife. With a semi-circular arc, the blade flashes down, over William's shoulder and into his heart. Silently, William slumps forward onto the table, his face crushed into the tools of his hobby. Below him, the wretched Pip whines. After a fraction of a second, the unknown assailant retreats. The concealed bookcase door closes behind him.

78 INT. DRAWING-ROOM. NIGHT.

Freddie returns. Jeremy makes to rise but Freddie stops him as Mabel comes over.

FREDDIE
No, no. Finish the hand.

MABEL
Where have you been?

FREDDIE
Never mind.

Now Anthony Meredith slides back into the room. In answer to Lavinia's enquiries, he just shakes his head reassuringly. George returns with the jug. Jennings speaks sharply under his breath.

JENNINGS
Well if that's a 'moment' I'd like to know what happens when you take a real break. Now give her ladyship some more coffee.

George takes the tray and approaches Sylvia. She holds out her cup.

SYLVIA
George, do you know what's become of Sir William?

GEORGE
I believe he's still in the library, milady.

(CONTINUED)

78 CONTINUED:

Louisa gets her refill. She is helping herself to milk and sugar so George is still and we can see Sylvia raising her eyebrows at her sister as she drops her voice.

SYLVIA
What *are* we going to do?

LOUISA
I could try and fetch him if you like.

SYLVIA
Would you, really? He much prefers you to me.

79 INT. UPSTAIRS HALL AND CORRIDOR / RED SALOON. NIGHT.

Mary, Probert and Lewis are still listening as Robert rejoins them. He carries two hot water bottles and hands one over to Mary. It is in a cover bearing the coronetted 'T.'

ROBERT
Here. I did yours as well. Before the rush starts.

Probert and Lewis acknowledge it is time to get to work. They walk away, past the door of the red saloon where we see Louisa. In front of her, Pip noses his way out of the almost closed library door and looks around. Louisa picks him up.

LOUISA
Come here you horrid little thing.
William, I -

But the rest of her speech is swallowed in a scream. At once, the music stops. The guests, followed by the different groups of listening servants, cluster into the red saloon. Isobel cranes forward but Rupert shields her until a sob from Probert brings them all to the door of the library. Mabel screams.

GEORGE
Bleedin' hell...

The body of Sir William McCordle is slumped over his work table. The eyes are open in the red face and the tongue is lolling out. It is clear that Sir William is very dead.

80 OMITTED

81 EXT. GOSFORD PARK. NIGHT.

A police car arrives. The driver, Constable Dexter, is joined by Inspector Thompson. Vain and clottish, he feels he belongs 'upstairs'. The house party will not agree.

82 INT. SERVANTS' HALL. NIGHT.

The servants are all seated round the table. Some of them, including Elsie, are in dressing-gowns. The atmosphere is mixed. The news is shocking but not particularly sad. Apart from Elsie and the upper servants, many of them, even the resident staff, hardly knew William except by sight. The 'front door' bell jangles on the bellboard.

JENNINGS
I'll go.

Jennings leaves. Elsie is sobbing aloud. Mrs Croft leans over and squeezes her hand. She speaks softly but loud enough for Bertha to hear her.

MRS CROFT
Come on, love. No man's worth it. At any rate, he isn't.

JANET
What are you going to do now, Mr Probert?

PROBERT
I don't know… I can't think straight…

GEORGE
When I leave here, I want to open a garage… Nothing gawdy. Just enough for a decent living.

RENEE
That's a funny ambition for a footman. Why aren't you a chauffeur?

LEWIS
I don't understand. Head footman in a house like this! You could be a butler if you play your cards right. And your future's taken care of!

BARNES
Future's taken care of? Don't make me laugh. Another twenty years and we'll have vanished like the Dodo.

(CONTINUED)

82 CONTINUED:

LEWIS
That's what they said in 1914 but here we still are.

Mary looks over at Robert, deep in thought. George follows her eyes.

GEORGE
You're very quiet. What's your ambition?

ROBERT
I don't think I've got one. Not now.

SARAH
I'm saving to open a hatshop. Very exclusive, regular clients…

GEORGE
Yes, I bet you'll have regular clients.

83 INT. UPSTAIRS HALL AND CORRIDOR./SALOON.

Weissman is on the telephone as Jennings crosses to the front door.

WEISSMAN
I don't understand… I thought they'd agreed it was a birdshoot… Why is fox hunting more cinematic? Who said that?…Oh… Well, OK, if it's a big deal, make it a fox hunt but what the hell are we doing here?

Jennings opens the door to the two policemen.

JENNINGS
We've been expecting you.

THOMPSON
Good evening. I'm Inspector Thomp –

Sylvia strides purposefully towards them, talking as she does so.

SYLVIA
You must be the police.

THOMPSON
Just so. I'm Inspector Thomp –

SYLVIA
I'm Lady Sylvia McCordle. We haven't moved him but I didn't know whether to ring for a doctor or not. William's real one's in London and it seemed very hard to wake him at this time of night.

THOMPSON
The police doctor will be here in a minute.

SYLVIA
Good. I mean I suppose it doesn't really matter if it's a stroke or a heart attack or whatever but we might as well get it right… Let's go straight to the red drawing-room. I've got everyone rounded up there.

Thompson glances at Weissman who is getting heated but Sylvia is in control.

SYLVIA (CONT'D)
Oh, don't mind him. He's just an American who's staying with us.

She has led them into the saloon, Jennings follows. All the upstairs members of the party are gathered in varying states of shock. Pip is in the corner, whining.

SYLVIA (CONT'D)
I'd better tell you who we all are then we can go to bed and leave you with poor William. Is that a good plan?

DEXTER
Do we need to worry them just now, sir? We could do it in the -

THOMPSON
Perhaps I should introduce myself. I'm Inspector Thomp –

SYLVIA
This is my aunt, Lady Trentham –

THOMPSON
Of course. The Countess of Trentham. How d'you do?
(MORE)

83 CONTINUED: (2)

THOMPSON (CONT'D)
I once had the pleasure of serving on a committee with the late Earl… I'm only sorry we have to meet in such tragic circumstances…

His pompous enunciating of Constance's full title tells her everything about his *petit bourgeois* origins. She wasn't aware that they were 'meeting' at all. Sylvia continues.

SYLVIA
My brother-in-law, Lord Stockbridge. My sister, Lady Stockbridge,...my youngest sister, Lady Lavinia Meredith, and her husband, Commander Meredith. Mr Novello, I suppose you knew that without my telling you...That'll be all, thank you Jennings...no, wait. Would you like to talk to any of the servants tonight, Inspector -

THOMPSON
Thomp –

SYLVIA
Perhaps you should see Probert. My poor husband's valet. Would you tell him to come up, Jennings? Now, where was I? This is Mr and Mrs Nesbitt, my daughter, Miss McCordle, Lord Rupert Standish and Mr Blond…

But Jennings has picked up Pip and left before she has finished the list.

84 INT. SERVANTS' HALL. NIGHT.

They are still seated as Jennings enters. He gives Pip to the odd man who takes the dog reluctantly. After a moment, Mrs Croft speaks.

MRS CROFT
Well? Don't leave us on tenterhooks.

JENNINGS
The police would like to see you for a moment, Mr Probert.

PROBERT
Me? Why? I don't know what I can tell them…

(CONTINUED)

84 CONTINUED:

But he goes, with a sigh and on the edge of tears, followed by sympathetic glances.

JENNINGS
There's no point in the rest of you waiting up.

ELSIE
What about me, Mr Jennings?

JENNINGS
You can leave as soon as the police release you. I dare say that'll be some time tomorrow.

MRS WILSON
Until then stay in your room.

ELSIE
I'm not contagious, you know.

BARNES
I'm sorry, Mr Jennings, but my two want to get away. So we'll be off early.

JENNINGS
Nobody's going anywhere... Now, those of you with remaining duties, see to them as quickly as you can. Otherwise, good night everyone.

He stands aside to let them pass. We hear some exchanges about the dog as they go. 'What's going to happen to it?' 'I should think she'll have it put down.''Best thing for it, nasty little beast.''No one can stand it except Sir William.' Alone among them, Elsie gives the animal a stroke. 'Don't do that, dear. He'll have your hand off.' While this is going on, Henry hesitates, unusually ill at ease.

JENNINGS (CONT'D)
Yes, Mr Weissman?

HENRY
I'm afraid I have a confession to make...

He speaks in an American accent.

85 INT. UPSTAIRS HALL AND CORRIDOR. NIGHT.

Probert walks mournfully past Weissman, still on the telephone.

(CONTINUED)

85 CONTINUED:

WEISSMAN
*Warner Olund wants cast approval?* Don't make me laugh! Warner Olund doesn't have the right to approve his own toilet!

86 INT. ELSIE'S ATTIC ROOM. NIGHT.

The two young women lie, trying to sleep. Elsie's half-packed case is visible.

MARY
I'm really sorry… about everything…

ELSIE
Don't feel sorry for me. Pity that poor Dorothy. She's got all the early morning teas to do, then trays *and* she's got to get Miss Isobel down to the dining-room – if she can find anything in black. I'm well out of it. She's the one who needs your sympathy.

MARY
I should think Miss Isobel might stay in bed tomorrow.

ELSIE
Unmarried girls don't have breakfast trays. Not at this house.

They are silent for a bit.

MARY
I wish I could help.

ELSIE
Well, you can't.

87 INT. STOCKBRIDGE BEDROOM. NIGHT

Renee is arranging the blanket cover on the bed. Behind her, Louisa sits at the dressing-table, wiping her eyes. In an open doorway, Raymond stands quite still as Robert slides his gown on and then comes round to set the lapels and tie the sash.

ROBERT
Is that everything, m'lord?

RAYMOND
Yes, thank you, Parks. I think we'd all better try and get some sleep.

(CONTINUED)

He nods at Renee and the two servants retire together, just in time to hear:

RAYMOND (CONT'D)
Do stop snivelling. Anyone would thing you were Italian.

88 INT. SALOON. NIGHT.

George is tidying up. He gives a cold glance over to where Henry is helping himself, Weissman and Novello to brandy from a tray. Ivor remarks his expression.

WEISSMAN
That's the main problem. Fox hasn't got anyone. Apart from a few washed-up silent stars… How are you getting on?

HENRY
Mrs Wilson's put me in the meanest room she could find.

IVOR
What did you expect? The State Bedchamber? You've made them feel like idiots. And they don't like it… Has anyone told Sylvia?

WEISSMAN
She'll be OK. She can take a joke.

Henry and Ivor exchange a look. They are not so sure.

IVOR
You'd better be the one to say it. I should go now. Before she hears it from someone else.

WEISSMAN
But don't tell her 'til afterwards. I wouldn't want to spoil it for her. Tonight of all nights.

His bitter tone does not merit an answer. Henry goes to the door. Weissman follows.

WEISSMAN (CONT'D)
Wait! I didn't mean that… Henry… will I see you later?

88 CONTINUED:

HENRY
I spent last night staring at the ceiling listening to the ramblings of a sleep-talking valet… I really think I need some rest, don't you?

He goes. Weissman turns disconsolately back into the room.

IVOR
That's not like you. Don't tell me you're jealous. He's not in the least interested, you know. He's just using you.

WEISSMAN
Why shouldn't he? I'm using him. It's a deal and I stick to my deals… I'm just surprised McCordle was right about her, that's all.

IVOR
I suppose a man knows his own wife. Besides, she has a point. Good-looking servants *are* the best. They don't dine with your friends.

89 INT. SYLVIA'S BEDROOM. NIGHT.

Sylvia, dry-eyed, lies on her bed as a sniffing Lewis goes round turning off the lights.

LEWIS
I'll say goodnight then, milady. Unless you'd like me stay with you?

Lewis goes. Sylvia crosses to the window. A noise tells her Henry has come in. He stands, hesitating to speak.

SYLVIA
What is it? Please tell me you haven't come with condolences.

She looks very beautiful and he is reluctant to jeopardise his fun.

HENRY
No, I - I was just wondering if you wanted some company.

He is Scottish again. She stares at him steadily for a moment before she answers.

(CONTINUED)

SYLVIA
Well… after all, I suppose life must go on…

90 INT. LIBRARY. NIGHT.

Probert is in tears. Dexter is sympathetic. Thompson is rather embarrassed.

THOMPSON
Try and pull yourself together, Mr Probert. I know it's hard but if you could be patient. They'll be here any minute…

PROBERT
Couldn't I just make him comfortable, sir? Please?

William, his face crushed into his tool collection, does look very *un*comfortable in his present position. Probert's grief has brought Ivor and Weissman to the door.

IVOR
Come on, Inspector.

DEXTER
It wouldn't be wise, sir. And it's not long to wai -

THOMPSON
Oh, very well. I don't suppose it can do any harm.

Probert takes hold of the dead man's shoulders. Is there a moment of tenderness? He gives a cry and the body falls back. As William's arms flop open and his head drops back, mouth gaping, his chest is revealed. The handle of the knife protrudes from it. By this time, Weissman has joined them. The five live men stare at the dead one.

THOMPSON (CONT'D)
Right. Well. Now you can see why we have the rules… Yes, Dexter? What is it?

DEXTER
Only that… there doesn't seem to be much blood, sir.

This is true and Thompson registers it. The fact is everything has changed.

90 CONTINUED:

IVOR
What happens next?

It's a good question.

91 EXT. GOSFORD PARK. EARLY MORNING.

The dawn of a new day. An undecorated hearse, laden with a coffin, drives away. The only sign of life is the small dog watching sadly from the steps.

92 INT. KITCHEN. EARLY MORNING.

The scullery maid blows on the range fire, trying to get it going. Bertha is laying out breakfast food. Ellen puts the silver entrée dishes in the warmer. Mrs Croft consults a menu book and writes her proposals for the day. Pip sniffs around.

BERTHA
George says Mr Novello was in on it. *And* Sir William. He says it was a joke on Lady Sylvia but I can't see that... The point is he's playing a butler in the next Charlie Chan and he wanted to make it authentic.

ELLEN
Well, he'd better not model his performance on Mr Jennings or they'll think he's as stiff as a board.

Their laughter is stilled as Thompson's head looks round the door. They all freeze, watching him. At first he faces the wrong way and so the room must appear empty to him. Then Ellen giggles and he spins round, stands and enters. Dexter is with him.

THOMPSON
Ah... Mrs Croft? I wonder if you could spare a few minutes. My name's Inspector Thomp –

MRS CROFT
I've no time for this now. I'm just doing the breakfast...

THOMPSON
It won't take long. Is there somewhere we could go? They're still cleaning upstairs... You can manage without her, I dare say?

(CONTINUED)

92 CONTINUED:

If this is a pleasantry, it falls on deaf ears. The others just watch him.

MRS CROFT
Well… I suppose you'd better come in here… Bertha, I'm leaving you in charge. Mind you see the menus go up on her ladyship's tray. And get that filthy dog out of here.

92A OMITTED

93 OMITTED

93A INT. MRS CROFT'S ROOM. DAY.

Mrs Croft has ushered Thompson into a cosy, little room at the back. He glances at an old tinted photograph of a baby in blue ribbons on her desk.

THOMPSON
My word, but you've a bonny lad there. What's he up to these days?

MRS CROFT
He's dead.

Once again, his jocularity has failed. He smiles nervously. Mrs Croft is quite cold.

MRS CROFT (CONT'D)
I don't know what I can tell you. Shouldn't you be looking for signs of a break-in?

THOMPSON
I gather there's no one here who's worked for Sir William longer than you have… Sad day…

94 INT. TRENTHAM BEDROOM. DAY.

Mary pours tea. On the tray, as we saw in 92A is a dish of sliced cucumber.

MARY
But why one of the knives from the silver pantry? Doesn't make sense.

94 CONTINUED:

CONSTANCE
He must have forgotten to bring one. And when you think what they have to carry about, all those gemmies and torches and skeleton keys… it's a miracle anyone ever gets burgled at all. It's worse than shooting. Anyway, it wasn't *in* the silver pantry. It's been missing since last night. Obviously, William had taken it and when the fellow surprised him, there it was on the table as handy as you like… By the way, are any of the others getting up for breakfast? The women, I mean.

MARY
I think Lady Lavinia may be.

CONSTANCE
That settles it. Come back at half past eight and I'll get dressed. The greatest bore of course but I don't want to miss anything.

She takes two of the slices of cucumber, lays them on her eyes and lies back.

94A INT. ISOBEL'S BEDROOM. DAY.

Isobel, in night things, is discussing it all with Elsie who is now in civilian clothes.

ISOBEL
But…do they know where he got in? Did he take anything?

ELSIE
No, but… I s'pose he ran for it… when he saw what he'd done… Are you going to be O.K.?

There is a knock. Elsie ducks behind the door as it opens on Dorothy.

DOROTHY
I wondered if you needed anything, miss…

ISOBEL
If you could just get a bath ready for me...

(CONTINUED)

94A CONTINUED:

The maid nods and closes the door. Isobel goes to a drawer and fetches an envelope.

ISOBEL (CONT'D)
When I came up last night I found this on my dressing-table.

ELSIE
What is it?

Isobel hands it over.

ELSIE (CONT'D)
'This is your final warning. If I have not received an offer from your father by luncheon tomorrow, I will tell him everything. Freddie.' Stupid idiot. At least he's off your back. That's something. He's got no one to tell now. At least, no one who'd give him a job to shut him up.

ISOBEL
You can't be sure. He might tell Rupert just for the fun of it… No doubt I'll hear from him soon enough.

The girl shrugs, limp with misery.

ELSIE
I'd better be off. I might not see you again. I'm only staying 'til the police give the nod.

ISOBEL
You're not in any… difficulty, are you?

ELSIE
Other than having no job and no home, you mean?

She relents, lightly stroking her stomach. Isobel, after all, has done her no harm.

ELSIE (CONT'D)
No. No worries there.

ISOBEL
I was forgetting. You're much cleverer than I was.

95 OMITTED

96 INT. BRUSHING ROOM. DAY.

Mary and Renee are working on some tweeds when Robert walks in carrying his employer's tweed suit.

MARY
I don't know why we're bothering. They're bound to cancel the shooting today.

ROBERT
Why?

The others are silenced for a moment by his response. Then:

MARY
I wonder what Lady Sylvia will do now.

RENEE
If I were her, I'd go to London. Set up as a glamorous widow with all the gentlemen chasing me for my money.

ROBERT
Not me. I grew up in London.

MARY
Is that where the orphanage was?

ROBERT
On the edge. Isleworth.

MARY
And you don't get homesick?

ROBERT
I don't think you're homesick if you've never had a home... Have you heard about Mr Weissman's valet?

RENEE
What about him?

ROBERT
Turns out he's a fraud. He isn't Scottish at all.

MARY
I could have told you that. Who is he, then?

96 CONTINUED:

A horrible thought strikes her.

MARY (CONT'D)
You don't think he's the murderer, do you?

ROBERT
Worse than that. He's an actor.

MRS WILSON
Your breakfast is ready in the Servants' Hall. After that the water should be hot enough for the baths.

How long has she been listening?

97 INT. UPSTAIRS HALL AND CORRIDOR. DAY.

Weissman is on the telephone which Thompson wants. Jennings is with them.

THOMPSON
I'm afraid I must insist…

WEISSMAN
I'll have to call you back. Don't go to sleep.

DEXTER
It might be more sensible if I drove you down to the village, sir.

THOMPSON
Thank you, Dexter. I know what I'm doing. This really is the only one, is it?

He is very important as he considers the exposed position of the implement.

JENNINGS
There's an extension in the servants' quarters. If you'd rather use that.

THOMPSON
I don't think so, thank you.

WEISSMAN
How long are you going to be?

97 CONTINUED:

THOMPSON
I have no idea… Hello? Yes, I want to place a Trunk Call. To London.

The camera moves away from him into a side corridor where Sarah stands listening.

98 INT. GALLERY. DAY.

Sarah, Renee and Barnes, carrying towels and bags are queuing at a door.

RENEE
You listened to the Inspector on the telephone? That's disgusting.

SARAH
I couldn't help it. I was just crossing the hall.

BARNES
So? What was he saying?

RENEE
Don't tell us. I don't want to know. It's eavesdropping.

But hers is not the consensus. And, at last, even Renee must admit she is curious.

RENEE (CONT'D)
Oh, go on, then.

SARAH
Well. He was talking to a lawyer in London. And it sounded to me as if Sir William had decided to change his –

The door opens and Isobel McCordle appears. The sight of her silences them.

SARAH (CONT'D)
I hope we didn't disturb you, miss… we're ever so sorry about…

Isobel just nods and hurries away. Barnes is starting to rinse and prepare the bath, when he sees Renee looking at her watch.

BARNES
What's the matter? Is yours in a hurry? Y'can go before me if you like.

98 CONTINUED:

RENEE
That's very kind. Are you sure? Won't Commander Meredith mind?

BARNES
Sod him. Let him wait. I don't care.

RENEE
Well, Sarah? Don't keep us in suspense.

Sarah continues to relay her findings as, a little way down the gallery, Lewis listens with interest.

99 INT. NESBITT BEDROOM. DAY.

Dorothy has brought Mabel's breakfast tray as Freddie comes in finishing his tie.

FREDDIE
Where's that George? Really, the slightest upset and these fellows go completely to pieces. How am I supposed to manage?

MABEL
Don't talk nonsense. You dress at home without any help.

FREDDIE
Well, I certainly never get any help from *you*.

MABEL
Pay no attention. He's in a bait and I know why.

She gives Dorothy a friendly wink.

100 INT. GALLERY/UPSTAIRS HALL AND CORRIDOR.

May passes with her box as the Merediths emerge. They start down the stairs as Barnes comes out of their room, just in time to hear what Anthony is saying.

ANTHONY
There is one thing: The bastard's death may have saved my bacon.

LAVINIA
For God's sake be quiet. What is the *matter* with you?

(CONTINUED)

100 CONTINUED:

Barnes's face assumes a look of power. He makes a V-sign at Anthony's back. As the Merediths reach the hall, Janet walks past Weissman who is on the telephone.

WEISSMAN
I know what time it is there… Of course I want you to wake him up. How else would you suggest I talk to him…? Is that you? Well… what did he say? *Clara Bow*? You're not serious. He wants to try *that* again!

The Merediths and Janet go towards the dining-room as Arthur arrives from downstairs carrying an entrée dish and opens the door.

101 INT. DINING-ROOM. DAY.

Rupert, Jeremy and Raymond are eating while Jennings stands by. Constance, choosing her food, looks up as the Merediths come in. The men read newspapers.

CONSTANCE
Good morning, dear. Have you heard? *Too* tiresome. That frightful inspector won't let anyone leave! So we're to be treated to another day of Mr Weissman shouting down the telephone.

IVOR
He has a problem with his work in Los Angeles, I'm afraid.

CONSTANCE
Well, he conducts his business very oddly. Coming down stairs just now, I thought I'd been transported to a bar in Marseilles.

Ivor doesn't contradict which is the right way to handle her.

CONSTANCE (CONT'D)
I gather they carted poor William off this morning. So strange and sad. Will they want to delay the funeral? I do hope it's not next week. I was meant to be with the de l'Isles and I was so looking forward to it.

IVOR
You must try not to upset yourself.

(CONTINUED)

Anthony and Raymond laugh which earns them a black look. Weissman comes in.

WEISSMAN
I have a call coming through and I want to take it no matter what.

JENNINGS
Very good, sir.

WEISSMAN
Now, could I have some eggs and is there any tomato?

JENNINGS
Of course, sir. Or perhaps you'd like to come and choose for yourself.

WEISSMAN
Oh? What? Cafeteria style?

At this, Raymond looks up from the paper he is reading as he eats.

RAYMOND
An Englishman is never waited on at breakfast.

WEISSMAN
Well, that's interesting because an American is.

He stands and goes to the sideboard, Thompson looks in, as gauche as ever.

THOMPSON
Ah. Good. Tell me, will Lady Sylvia be down soon?

CONSTANCE
I shouldn't think so. She has breakfast in her room and then she usually goes for a ride.

THOMPSON
Possibly. But I doubt she will this morning.

He is very assured but their expressions tell us that they do not agree.

101 CONTINUED: (2)

THOMPSON (CONT'D)
In that case… Lady Trentham, I wonder if I might have a few words? We're in the library. Whenever you're ready.

CONSTANCE
If you wish, Inspector. I'm afraid I won't be much help… but I suppose on a day like this we all have to pull our weight.

The door opens and Isobel enters. Her black frock and air of sadness cast a pall on the room. Rupert jumps up to help her with breakfast and Jeremy looks on.

102 EXT. KITCHEN COURT. DAY.

Robert is emerging from the laundry. In one corner of the yard is a game larder. Ellen is there holding some birds and Bertha comes out with more. She nods at Robert.

ROBERT
Do you want a hand?

He relieves her of some of the birds as Pip jumps up at them.

ROBERT (CONT'D)
Get away! Ugh. These smell as if they could walk in on their own. I don't know how they can eat them like that.

ELLEN
You heard Mr Denton's made a right chump out of Mr Jennings.

BERTHA
Never mind that. What about Sir William? Apparently he wasn't stabbed after all. I mean he was but that's not why he died… He was poisoned. That's what killed him. The Inspector told Mrs Croft. They don't know why the killer stabbed him as well but he must have been dead already. That's why there was no blood. Dead bodies don't bleed, you know.

Robert looks at her. She's awfully proud to have the facts. Ellen bursts out laughing.

(CONTINUED)

102 CONTINUED:

ELLEN
Trust Sir William to be murdered *twice*.

103 INT. BUTLER'S PANTRY. DAY.

George and Arthur, supervised by Jennings, clean the huge centrepiece with various tools. Among these, one jar is labelled poison. Probert watches but does not help.

ARTHUR
Did he say anything about changing his will, Mr Probert?

PROBERT
Not in so many words...

They all look at the valet. Clearly he does know something whatever he says.

PROBERT (CONT'D)
Well, I remember him looking at a picture of her ladyship a week or two ago... the one on the tallboy in his dressing-room where she's laughing... Anyway, he said 'her nose is due for re-setting' and I said 'why' and he said 'cos it's about to go out of joint.'

ARTHUR
Except it isn't.

GEORGE
Exactly.

ARTHUR
Why do you think he was murdered, Mr Jennings?

JENNINGS
Don't talk nonsense. Of course he wasn't murdered! Not like that. Some ruffian broke in, thinking the library was empty, Sir William surprised him and paid the price for it. And very tragic it is, too.

(CONTINUED)

103 CONTINUED:

GEORGE
I can't see that, Mr Jennings. I mean, I don't think ruffians go about poisoning people and then stabbing their corpses. Apart from anything else, they're usually in a bit of a hurry.

JENNINGS
What are you suggesting?

GEORGE
I'm not suggesting anything. Just...

JENNINGS
Just what?

GEORGE
Well, it looks to me like Sir William was killed by someone who meant to do it. That's all. No wonder they won't let anyone leave. Tough luck on whoever's got any secrets to hide...

JENNINGS
If you can only talk rubbish, George, I suggest you don't talk at all.

George's tone was almost jocular. Jennings's is not. George catches Arthur's eye.

104 INT. KITCHEN. DAY.

Mrs Croft is in the kitchen with the others.

MRS CROFT
Right. They've cancelled the shooting so Muggins here's got to pull a dining-room luncheon for God knows how many out of the hat...Is her Ladyship back yet?

BERTHA
No.

MRS CROFT
Then she'll have to take what she's given.

ETHEL
I dunno... Why would anyone want to kill Sir William?

104 CONTINUED:

MRS CROFT
Well he wasn't Father Christmas.

This gets the attention of all the girls which she shrugs off.

MRS CROFT (CONT'D)
He made a few enemies in his time.

LOTTIE
What d'you mean, "enemies"? When?

BERTHA
Was this before the war? When you were a factory worker?

MRS CROFT
Excuse me, I was *not* a factory worker. I was *never* a factory worker. I was a *cook* in one of his factories. He had four, two in Isleworth and two in Twickenham. And all full of girls so you can imagine...

ELLEN
But wasn't it risky? With factory girls? Suppose they'd complained?

MRS CROFT
Who to, exactly?

BERTHA
But suppose they got...?

MAUD
Got what?

MRS CROFT
I don't know why *you're* looking so shocked. Didn't happen that often but if it did, he'd arrange an adoption.

BERTHA
But if you didn't want it adopted? If you wanted to keep it?

MRS CROFT
Then you lost your job. Kicked out. You take my word for it. He was a hard-hearted randy old sod.

ELLEN
So the business with Elsie...

(CONTINUED)

104 CONTINUED: (2)

MRS CROFT
Just shows a leopard never changes his spots. Now come on the rest of you. Just because Sir William's died doesn't mean the clock's stopped.

105 EXT. KITCHEN COURT. DAY.

Lewis stands in the back entrance watching as her mistress canters into the yard. To the maid's surprise, Raymond steps out of the shadows. He hurries to Sylvia as she dismounts. We can only just hear that Sylvia is indignant. "Why shouldn't I? I wanted some air." Raymond appears to be remonstrating as soon as the groom leads the horse away. Drawn by curiosity, Lewis edges nearer until she is within earshot.

RAYMOND
They seem to be asking a whole lot of questions about things that can't possibly have anything to do with William's death… and I thought…

He hesitates, noticing the approaching maid.

SYLVIA
Never mind Lewis. The Seal of the Confessional's got nothing on her. Has it, Lewis?

LEWIS
I should hope *not*, milady.

Sylvia smiles at her indignation, addressing Raymond in a stage whisper.

SYLVIA
She's rather anti-Catholic… So?

RAYMOND
It's only that the police seem to be raking about, looking for their grubby motives, and I don't want them muddled with with silly tales from the distant past...

SYLVIA
But darling, you're quite safe. I'm sure it's not illegal. Even for someone who does it as badly as you do.

(CONTINUED)

105 CONTINUED:

She shares this with Lewis who, despite the personal morality of a Carmelite nun, delights in her mistress's defeat of a mere man.

RAYMOND
That's *exactly* what I'm talking about. You say things to be funny that can't be *un*said...And it's not important.

SYLVIA
But isn't it for them to say what's important and what isn't? Yes, Lewis? What is it?

LEWIS
The Inspector's been asking for you, milady, and I wanted you to know… he's been talking to the lawyers in London...

SYLVIA
Has he, indeed? Well, he'll have to wait. I want a bath. Who's in the firing line at the moment?

LEWIS
I think Lady Trentham's in the library just now, milady.

SYLVIA
God help them.

106 INT. LIBRARY. DAY.

Mary is by the door. Thompson has been talking to Constance. Dexter is an observer.

THOMPSON
Ah, come in Miss Maceachhh… er… I'm Inspector Thomp –

CONSTANCE
There you are, Mary. This is all too tiresome and absurd. They're making the greatest fuss over –

THOMPSON
If you don't mind – I've some questions I'd like to ask the young lady.

(CONTINUED)

106 CONTINUED:

CONSTANCE
Well, I'm certainly not leaving if that's what you think.

Thompson looks to Dexter. This is just the kind of woman he could do without.

THOMPSON
Would it bother you if Lady Trentham stays?

MARY
Why should it?

THOMPSON
No reason. Only… we understand that there may have been some difficulty between the late Sir William McCordle and your employer –

CONSTANCE
Really, this is too vulgar almost to be believed –

MARY
I wasn't aware of that, sir. They got on well as far as I could see.

Constance relaxes with a superior smile at Thompson as he flails about.

THOMPSON
So you weren't conscious of any trouble over an allowance? An allowance, I might add, that Sir William's death has now made secure.

MARY
What sort of an allowance would that be, sir?

Constance regards the girl with far more interest than she has ever done before.

107 INT. IRONING AND SEWING ROOM. DAY.

Dorothy is mending a black dress. She looks up. Jennings is in the doorway.

JENNINGS
I wondered who was in here. I hope you've got enough light for that.
(MORE)

(CONTINUED)

107 CONTINUED:

JENNINGS (CONT'D)
Black on black. Don't want you going blind on top of everything else.

DOROTHY
Miss Isobel's only got two black frocks and this one's torn.

JENNINGS
I'm sorry the business with Elsie's landed you with so much work. That's what you get for being so reliable.

This comment, simply meant, lights a fire in Dorothy's soul.

DOROTHY
Never mind me… Have you spoken to the police again?

JENNINGS
Not yet…

DOROTHY
I suppose they have to ask their questions.

JENNINGS
Oh yes…

DOROTHY
Will they be talking to all of us?

JENNINGS
I shouldn't think so...Well, I'll leave you to it. I could ask Miss Lewis to give you a hand with that if you like...

Plainly he is distracted with some sort of worry. She looks at him tenderly.

DOROTHY
No need. It's nearly done… Mr Jennings… You know I'd say anything you want me to.

JENNINGS
What?

DOROTHY
Anything at all. I don't care what I tell them. If it'll help. You know that, don't you? You've only to ask.

(CONTINUED)

107 CONTINUED: (2)

Her face has never been more suffused with feeling. Jennings is horrified to be confronted with this unwanted declaration of love.

108 INT. LIBRARY. DAY.

George is arranging tea on a table for Thompson, Dexter and Sylvia.

THOMPSON
No. The point I'm trying to make is only that if he *had* signed it, then your position would have been quite altered.

SYLVIA
I suppose so. But he didn't.

THOMPSON
Precisely… May I pour you some tea?

In his brain, he is Poirot as he reaches down and picks up the milk jug.

SYLVIA
How kind you are. But could you bear to put my milk in afterwards?

She smiles, enjoying his *gaffe* as he clumsily replaces the jug and picks up the pot.

109 INT. JENNINGS'S ROOM. DAY.

Gathered at the door, the servants listen to Jennings.

JENNINGS
I assume, by this time, you all know that Mr Denton has played a trick on us in posing as a valet. Since Sir William was aware of the plan, it is not for me, or any of you, to criticise it. However, it leaves us with a few adjustments to make for this evening. Arthur, you can take over dressing Mr Weissman. Which leaves us with the problem of Mr Novello. I really don't want to ask Mr Probert.

ARTHUR
I don't mind, Mr Jennings.

109 CONTINUED:

JENNINGS
No, you've got enough on your plate.

Arthur's hopes are dashed again. Robert looks up.

ROBERT
I'll do him if you like.

JENNINGS
That's very generous of you, Mr Stockbridge. Otherwise, I could always do him, myself.

ROBERT
No, no. It's no trouble. It's only for a night or two.

JENNINGS
Good. That's settled then. And I think Mr Denton can dress himself. Thank you all. You can go.

With Lewis muttering 'cheeky beggar,' they file out leaving only Probert and Mrs Wilson. Jennings goes to a table where he has a bottle of port, a decanter, a glass and a funnel. He starts to open and then taste and decant the port with care.

JENNINGS (CONT'D)
I'm giving them a glass of the 1912 tonight. They'll need a bit of cheering up.

MRS WILSON
What about you, Mr Probert? How are you getting on? Have you made any plans yet?

PROBERT
I think I'll go to my sister's for a week or two. Sort something out. I've an idea she and I might open a little hotel together, well, a B and B really. We've talked about it and this might be the moment…

MRS WILSON
What? You mean you won't stay on in service? I am surprised.

(CONTINUED)

109 CONTINUED: (2)

JENNINGS
Are you Mrs Wilson? When every day one reads of another house sold as a school or demolished to make way for a hospital? Maybe Mr Probert's right. Maybe we're nothing but a race of dinosaurs...

He smiles sadly at his little joke. His next words confirm this is the end of an era.

JENNINGS (CONT'D)
As a matter of fact, I too may be leaving here soon.

MRS WILSON
I very much hope not.

JENNINGS
Me too. Me too… but one is not Always in control of these things…and please don't concern yourself. Believe me, I have fully deserved whatever comes.

MRS WILSON
There are worse people than you in this house.

110 INT. BOOT ROOM. DAY.

Robert and Mary are cleaning evening shoes. They wear aprons and gloves.

ROBERT
Certainly they'll give her a good reference. Otherwise they'd have to explain why they were giving her a bad one.

This makes her smile. She gets her nerve up.

MARY
Mr Parks -

ROBERT
Robert.

She is torn between pleasure at this mark of his regard and the question that's been troubling her.

110 CONTINUED:

MARY
Robert, then...it's just...when you said, last night, that you'd surprise me...you didn't mean anything by it, did you?

ROBERT
What do you think?

MARY
Don't frighten me.

ROBERT
Why? Don't you like surprises?

ROBERT (CONT'D)
Better get cracking. I've got two grown men to dress.

He stands, taking off the apron. Then he reaches out and gives a soft pinch to her cheek.

111 INT. LIBRARY/UPSTAIRS HALL AND CORRIDOR. DAY.

Barnes, the valet, is being questioned.

THOMPSON (VO)
"The bastard's death may have saved my bacon..." What do you think he meant by that?

BARNES
Isn't it obvious?

Nothing is obvious to Thompson.

THOMPSON
Is it?

DEXTER
Perhaps he meant that the investment Sir William had agreed would have to be paid now. By the executors or who-

THOMPSON
What about the low shot that was fired when they were out that morning? Do you think it might have been intended for Sir William?

BARNES
Well, it nearly took his ear off.

111 CONTINUED:

THOMPSON
Thank you, Mr Barnes. You've been very helpful. Now, perhaps you would ask Captain Meredith to join us.

BARNES
You won't… tell him what I said, will you, Inspector – ?

THOMPSON
*Thompson*. My name is Inspector *Thompson*. Now please fetch him down.

Barnes, slightly unnerved by the anger he has released, retreats. As he closes the door, we can hear Weissman on the telephone. Barnes walks past him through the hall.

WEISSMAN
You tell me: Who is Ray Milland? O.K. but no Clara Bow, no Janet Gaynor. Tell him I'll sign Milland if we can be free of the un-dead… No, the study was fine. No the shoot-out in the study is fine. Yes, I'm sure. Philip may be writing it but I'm *living* it. The stables? Why would anyone be murdered in the stables?… What is it with Sheehan and these fucking horses?

112 INT. KITCHEN CORRIDOR. EVE.

George is smoking and gossiping with Arthur. Nearby May and Janet are unloading coal scuttles full of a mixture of coal and debris from the upstairs fires. The men make no effort to help.

ELSIE
Pssst!

They look up. Elsie is above them on the stairs. Again, she is wearing her own clothes.

GEORGE
They'll be coming in a minute. The dressing bell's just gone.

ELSIE
I'm going mad up there… I've read all me magazines twice over…You couldn't pinch one from the library, could you? I don't care if it's "Horse and Hound" so long as I haven't read it.

(CONTINUED)

Renee, Sarah, Barnes, Mary and Robert are in the corridor, carrying bits of clothing.

RENEE
What's yours wearing? We've only got dark green...

SARAH
I don't think mine's bothered. She hasn't got any black here, anyway.

MARY
Funny lot, aren't they? When you think about it. Changing for dinner on a day like this –

She breaks off as Henry Denton appears, behind Elsie, on the stairs. There is a pause.

BARNES
Well. *We are* honoured. In case you've forgotten, this is the servants' area. Sir. Yours is on the other side of the door at the top, there. Sir.

HENRY
It was just... I wanted to explain...

GEORGE
No explanation's necessary, Mr Denton, now if you'll excuse us, we have work to do. Come on, Arthur.

The footmen take the scuttles and go. The others push past him. Robert is the last.

HENRY
Robert, surely... It was just a laugh...

ROBERT
Then perhaps you'd better enjoy your laugh in the drawing-room, sir.

He speaks without malice but, having spoken, he too is gone. Elsie speaks.

ELSIE
They're afraid you'll repeat things. That you won't be discreet.

112 CONTINUED: (2)

HENRY
But I'm very discreet. That's what I'm known for. My discretion.

ELSIE
You never give up, do you?

113 INT. GALLERY. EVE.

Robert is walking down the gallery. He hears voices coming from an open doorway.

ISOBEL
You can tell him but he won't give you any money...and Mummy wouldn't pay five pounds to save me from the gallows...

FREDDIE
Don't keep talking as if I was enjoying this. What I *wanted* was a job...

As Robert reaches them, by Isobel's door, they are silent. Then, after he has passed:

ISOBEL
My chequebook's in the library. I'll do it after dinner.

Freddie leaves as Robert is hailed by Raymond at the far end of the gallery. Before the valet can reach him, Raymond sees Anthony approach, looking haggard.

RAYMOND
You look as if you've had rather a pasting.

ANTHONY
They kept on and on about that low shot yesterday...They wouldn't let it go. I *told* them it was nothing to do with me.

RAYMOND
I'm sure you did. But another time, Anthony, try to be less greedy.

Before Anthony can protest, Raymond addresses Robert who's nearly reached them.

113 CONTINUED:

RAYMOND (CONT'D)
Ah, Parks. Can you see to Mr Novello first? I want to have a word with her ladyship.

With a quick "very good, m'lord", Robert moves off. Anthony has been hovering, trying to get a word in.

ANTHONY
Raymond, I don't know why you -

RAYMOND
I saw you. Of course it was an accident. When a man's as short as you are, it must be hard to gauge the height of the birds. But, next time, do be more careful. Please.

His tone is quite dismissive as he goes into the room and shuts the door, leaving Anthony completely humiliated in front of the valet.

114 INT. TRENTHAM BEDROOM. EVE.

Constance is finishing her toilet with Mary's help.

MARY
You heard he was cutting Lady Sylvia out in favour of Miss Isobel?

CONSTANCE
That's nothing. Wait for *this*...in the new will he'd left Lady Stockbridge a *hundred thousand pounds*. Can you imagine? Sylvia thinks it's a huge joke. Particularly since she won't have to pay it.

MARY
But were they...?

CONSTANCE
Well, as the saying goes, the time to make up your mind about people is *never*... Which reminds me, I haven't complimented you on how you managed those horrible little men in the library... I've been thinking, Mary. You're not a trainee any more. It's time your salary reflected your skills. We'll talk about it when we get home.

(CONTINUED)

114 CONTINUED:

The power balance, between these two has been quite altered by the last 24 hours.

115 INT. NOVELLO BEDROOM/GALLERY. EVE.

Robert crouches on the floor holding a shoe horn inside the back of a pair of evening pumps as a black-socked foot enters the frame and is guided into the shoe.

IVOR (VO)
He was an odd mixture. Better and worse than people thought him. It's strange but he always seemed to me the luckiest man I'd ever met… until now. I wonder what his star sign was.

Robert stands and starts to brush Ivor's tails. He speaks without thinking.

ROBERT
Gemini, sir.

IVOR
How on earth do you know that?

Robert picks up two shirts and some underwear.

ROBERT
I think I'd better have these washed, sir. They still won't say how long you're going to be here.

116 INT. STOCKBRIDGE BEDROOM. DAY.

With a swift know, Renee opnes the door. A savage row is in progress.

RAYMOND
*Don't lie to me, you bitch!*

Suddenly they are aware of the maid. There is a frozen moment. Until:

RENEE
Lady Lavinia won't be in black, milady. So we should be all right. But we ought to get started…

With a supreme effort, Raymond regains control. He walks to the door.

116 CONTINUED:

RAYMOND
We'll talk about it later.

LOUISA
If you like. I've got nothing else to say.

RAYMOND
I just want you to be honest with me.

LOUISA
Do you Raymond? And suppose I want you to be honest with me?

117 INT. SERVANTS' HALL. EVE.

Barnes, Probert and the other valets and ladies' maids are relaxing. The boy is wiping down the table after the servants' dinner. Jennings looks in.

JENNINGS
You don't know where Commander Meredith might have got to, do you?

BARNES
No.

JENNINGS
Only he's never come downstairs and he's not in his room.

BARNES
Mr. Jennings, I have washed him and dressed him. If he can't find his way to the drawing room, it's not my fault.

JENNINGS
Well, we can't delay dinner much longer.

BARNES
Then he'll have to go hungry, won't he?

The others are torn between shock and amusement. Pip wanders up to Barnes' chair and he savagely kicks him away. Probert looks at Jennings and raises his brows.

118 INT. STILL ROOM. NIGHT.

Dorothy comes in with a tray of things for the morning. She starts. Sitting alone in the darkness, is Anthony Meredith. He is in evening dress.

DOROTHY
I'm sorry, sir. I didn't mean to disturb you...

ANTHONY
No, no. Please... Come in... I'm afraid I'm in your way...

DOROTHY
No... it's no bother... Are you all right, sir?

ANTHONY
I've been questioned by the Inspector... I feel a little bruised.

He glances out of the dark window. When he speaks, he does not turn to her.

ANTHONY (CONT'D)
Why is it, would you say, that some people seem to get whatever they want in life? Everything they touch turns to gold... While others can strive and strive... and have nothing...

He looks across with a face devoid of hope. Still she stands, listening.

ANTHONY (CONT'D)
I wonder... Do you believe in luck? Do you think some men are lucky and some just... aren't, and there's nothing they can do about it?

Dorothy ponders for a moment. Of course he has asked her own question.

DOROTHY
I believe in love. Not just getting it... giving it. I think as long as you can love somebody, whether or not they love you, then it's worth it...

For a moment the defeated duo look at each other. The Master and the Maid. He nods.

118 CONTINUED:

ANTHONY
Good answer… I'd better go up. They must have finished dinner by now… Thank you…

He is gone.

119 INT. DRAWING-ROOM. NIGHT.

The mood is subdued. Constance, Louisa, Lavinia and Raymond are playing bridge. George takes the coffee tray to Isobel and Rupert at one end of the room.

ISOBEL
If only I could believe you...

RUPERT
I wish you would.

George moves on to Sylvia who is reading a magazine. Henry sits near her.

HENRY
There's an article in that on Blenheim. Are you interested in houses?

SYLVIA
Not very.

She answers without looking up. Behind, Ivor plays "Keep the Home Fires Burning".

MABEL
Oh, how that tune used to make me cry.

Turning to say this, her eye is caught by Isobel handing something to Freddie by the door. Louisa speaks from the card table as she takes a drink from Jennings.

LOUISA
Couldn't you play something a little more cheerful, Mr Novello? We're all quite emotional enough as it is.

Ivor obliges, moving into waltz time. Weissman leans over to him as Jennings arrives.

WEISSMAN
That's if they have emotions.

(CONTINUED)

119 CONTINUED:

IVOR
You're too hard on them. Don't you agree, Jennings?

JENNINGS
Sir?

IVOR
Mr Weissman is criticising the aristocracy but he wouldn't if he'd been here during the war, would he, instead of lazing about in California? We admired their stiff upper lips then, didn't we, Jennings?

JENNINGS
Much more than I realised at the time, sir.

His voice is choked with emotion. Surprised at the intensity he has provoked, Ivor nods at Weissman with raised brows.

IVOR
See.

Mabel and Freddie are talking softly as Jennings arrives back at the drinks table.

MABEL
What was Isobel giving you just now?

FREDDIE
I don't know what you mean.

She holds out her hand as Anthony enters. Sylvia looks up and returns to her reading.

LOUISA
Anthony. There you are. Where have you been? You're too late for dinner but I'm sure they can bring you a tray if you're hungry.

ANTHONY
No. I don't want anything, thank you…

LAVINIA
Isobel, come and take over will you?

As she goes to Anthony, Henry jumps up. George has tipped a coffee pot over him.

119 CONTINUED: (2)

GEORGE
I do apologise, sir. I can't think how that happened.

120 INT. SERVANTS' HALL. NIGHT.

A wireless plays music. Arthur is practising dance steps with Ellen. Mary and Robert listen while Dexter drinks tea. Lewis mends lace, Sarah and Renee sew by the fire. Bertha is scraping out scallop shells with a wire brush. Barnes reads. Probert has a leather collar box and he is sorting collars into sizes. Pip hovers.

BERTHA
What's the point of that, Mr Probert? Won't it all be chucked out?

PROBERT
I'll know I've left it in good order. It's all I can do for him now.

ROBERT
Leave him alone.

Barnes glances at Bertha scraping away as Mrs Wilson looks in.

BARNES
I wish you'd stop that. It's making my teeth go funny.

BERTHA
I can't help that. Put that dog out someone.

MRS WILSON
Constable, I'm glad I've caught you. I'm assuming that the Inspector won't keep everyone beyond tomorrow but I thought I'd check with you.

DEXTER
Well...we haven't spoken to all the serv
-

Thompson looks in.

THOMPSON
There you are, Dexter. Come along. We're going home.

120 CONTINUED:

MRS WILSON
I was just asking the Constable how long our guests will be staying. Only Mrs Croft has the meals to arrange and one of the housemaids is anxious to get away…

THOMPSON
Oh that'll be all right. I'm not bothered about the servants. Just the people who might have had a real connection with the dead man.

The others watch Mrs Wilson. They are interested to see how she answers.

MRS WILSON
I see… yes, I suppose you would be.

THOMPSON
Still, I think they can go home. We've got their addresses after all. Dexter will come in tomorrow to confirm it. But don't worry...It won't end there. I'll find him. Whoever he is. I always do.

He leaves. Before Dexter can follow him, Bertha speaks.

BERTHA
Does he?

Dexter hesitates.

DEXTER
It's been known.

121 OMITTED

122 OMITTED

123 INT. IRONING AND SEWING ROOM. NIGHT.

George enters. There is a sound of scuffling. He turns on the light. Bertha is on the floor with Jeremy Blond. In silence the latter stands, tucking in his shirt and fastening his fly buttons. He refuses to make the smallest gesture of embarrassment.

GEORGE
Right. Beg your pardon, sir. I was just collecting Mr Nesbitt's shirts.

123 CONTINUED:

Without a word, Jeremy leaves. George looks at Bertha. After a moment, they both dissolve into giggles.

GEORGE (CONT'D)
You naughty, naughty girl.

BERTHA
Poor bloke. We were in 'ere on Tuesday and one of the visiting maids walked in. He must think I did it on purpose.

She goes to the door as George is taking some shirts from one of the great cupboards.

BERTHA (CONT'D)
You won't tell, will you?

GEORGE
I won't tell. But you're lucky you're in the kitchen and not under Mrs Wilson. She'd sniff it out without any help from me.

124 INT. SYLVIA'S BEDROOM. NIGHT.

Lewis is settling Sylvia for the night when they both hear the door opening. Henry stands there. Sylvia continues to read her book. Lewis takes her cue.

LEWIS
Will that be all, milady?

SYLVIA
Don't go, Lewis. There's no need.

She ignores the hapless Henry until he is provoked into something like anger.

HENRY
I just don't see what's changed!

Sylvia at last takes her eyes from the page.

SYLVIA
Then you are a fool as well as a liar.

124A INT. STILL ROOM. NIGHT

Dorothy is wiping the surfaces at the end of a long day. Mrs Wilson looks in.

124A CONTINUED:

MRS WILSON
Quickly. I need your help.

125 INT. SERVANTS' HALL. NIGHT.

The room is dark. The sole occupant, Jennings, is slumped onto the central table. A glass and an empty bottle are near his hand. Mrs Wilson and Dorothy hurry in.

MRS WILSON
We have to get him to his own room. Nobody must see him like this.

DOROTHY
Don't you worry, Mr Jennings. Everything's all right.

With a massive effort, they get him upright and half walk, half drag him to the door.

126 INT. JENNING'S BEDROOM. NIGHT.

The two women, seriously dishevelled by their efforts, struggle in with the nearly unconscious man. They dump him onto the bed and set to work.

MRS WILSON
Take his shoes off while I loosen his collar… There. Now go to bed and don't say anything about this.

Dorothy kisses her finger and secretly presses it to the forehead of the sleeping man.

127 INT. ELSIE'S ATTIC ROOM. NIGHT.

Mary is in bed. Her valise is open on the chest. She is watching while Elsie packs a battered case which is on her bed.

ELSIE
So George got his own back on Mr Denton. Good.

MARY
He gave me the creeps.

There is a light knock and Isobel enters.

ISOBEL
You're still here then.

127 CONTINUED:

ELSIE
Only 'till the morning.

Isobel nods. She hesitates to speak looking at Mary.

ELSIE (CONT'D)
Don't worry about her. What is it?

ISOBEL
I...I thought you'd like to know that
Mabel Nesbitt left this on my dressing-
table...I think it's over.

She hands Elsie an envelope with the torn cheque and a note.
Elsie nods, pleased.

ISOBEL (CONT'D)
And I just wanted to be certain...You
never did speak to Daddy about it that
night? About Freddie and everything?

ELSIE
I told you. I never had a moment...

ISOBEL
No, I'm glad...that he wasn't bothered
with it before he...Well...I suppose
I'd better go...Good luck, Elsie.

ELSIE
Good luck to you, Miss.

A thoughtful Elsie holds the door as Isobel slips away. Mary
looks curiously at her companion.

ELSIE (CONT'D)
Don't ask.

MARY
Do you think Sir William was in love
with you?

ELSIE
Nah. I was a bit of fun, that's all.

MARY
What about you?

ELSIE
I didn't love him but... I didn't mind
'im... I liked the way he'd talk.
(MORE)

127 CONTINUED: (2)

ELSIE (CONT'D)
He only talked to me 'cos he was sick of 'er but I liked it. He used to tell me I could be anything I wanted... if I wanted it enough...

MARY
You're not sorry, then. Even with the way it's turned out.

ELSIE
No. I'm not sorry... it's time for a change. Who knows? Might be the making of me. What was it 'e used to say? Carpe Diem. Sieze the day.

This strikes a chord with Mary. She gets out of bed and puts on her dressing-gown.

ELSIE (CONT'D)
What's up? What have I said? Where are you off to?

128 INT. ROBERT'S ATTIC ROOM. NIGHT.

Robert is sitting on his bed. The door opens. It is Mary. He is dumbfounded.

ROBERT
What are you doing here?

But she is silent, trembling in her sad little, candlewick dressing-gown.

ROBERT (CONT'D)
You'd better get back to your room. They mustn't find you up here.

For a moment, she cannot decide if she wants to put the next question.

MARY
You didn't really dislike him, did you...? Not really...? At least... not enough to kill him...

But he says nothing. Her eyes fill.

MARY (CONT'D)
You can't have! You didn't know him! You'd have to hate him and why would you?

She is so desperate that he should not be guilty. Robert's eyes meet hers

ROBERT
Can't a man hate his own father?

Mary could scarcely be more shocked if he'd hit her. She stares at him.

ROBERT (CONT'D)
Sir William McCordle was my father. He didn't know it. But he was.

MARY
But... you said you were an orphan...

ROBERT
I said I grew up in an orphanage.

Now he decides to tell a little bit of the truth.

ROBERT (CONT'D)
Not long before I left, a group of us got into the Warden's office one night. We unpicked the lock and took out our files. It was a prank, really. I didn't expect any shocking discoveries. Just a birth certificate with my mother's name and 'father unknown'. This picture was with it.

She takes the picture and studies it.

MARY
But how did Sir William come into it?

ROBERT
They had my admission form. I was two days old. Guess who brought me to the door.

MARY
But that doesn't mean –

ROBERT
Yes it does. After that, I found out. She was a factory worker. She wasn't the only one... either the authorities didn't know or they didn't want to know. They took the babies and they took his donations.

MARY
What happened to her?

ROBERT
I asked them once. She died. When I was little… I always say she died of a broken heart but it was probably cyrrosis of the liver… "Broken heart" sounds a bit nicer, don't you think?

MARY
Is that why you took the job with Lord Stockbridge? To get to Sir William? To poison him?

ROBERT
I didn't poison him.

MARY
What?

ROBERT
I didn't poison him.

This is wonderful news.

MARY
But then you didn't kill him...Tell me you didn't stab him either.

At this he is silent. Nevertheless it is still good news.

MARY (CONT'D)
I know you didn't. I'm sure you didn't...Even if you did, that didn't kill him. And whoever did it knew that. No one could stab a corpse and not know it.

ROBERT
Is that right? When did you last stab a corpse?

MARY
But...who really murdered him?

ROBERT
I don't know. And I don't care.

With those words, she knows her theory is correct. The mood has altered between them. He comes to her. When he takes her in his arms, she does not resist his kiss.

128 CONTINUED: (3)

ROBERT (CONT'D)
I've been wanting to do that since I first set eyes on you.

129 INT. HENRY'S BEDROOM. EARLY MORNING.

The morning light glints through the drawn curtains. The door opens softly and Janet, the little housemaid, wearing a long, 'kneeling' apron and carrying a bucket of coal tiptoes to the fire. She puts on thick, felt gloves and sets to work.

HENRY (VO)
Who is it?

The voice startles the girl. She turns. He sits up.

JANET
I'm ever so sorry, sir.

HENRY
Sorry for what?

JANET
I'm supposed to get the fire lit without waking you.

HENRY
Why does everyone treat me as if I was just one of the guests? I spent half the week downstairs with you all.

JANET
But you can't be on both teams at once, sir.

HENRY
More's the pity.

He is sad as he watches her light the fire. With a nervous bob, she hurries out.

130 INT. MRS CROFT'S ROOM. DAY.

Mrs Croft is at her desk. Bertha looks in.

BERTHA
It's official. They're off after breakfast. The constable told me.

MRS CROFT
Well, thank God for that. What about him?

(CONTINUED)

130 CONTINUED:

Together they look through the glass of Mrs Croft's office to where Dexter hovers in the corridor.

BERTHA
He's going too. Soon as he's seen Mr Jennings... Did you tell them any of that stuff in the end?

MRS CROFT
I did not. I'm sorry if I shock you, Bertha, but the plain fact is he only got what he deserved. There. I've said it.

BERTHA
I can't stop thinking about those girls…the ones that got...you know...

MRS CROFT
I don't wonder at it. The way you carry on. Just make sure it never happens to you, my girl.

She is severe but not unkind. It is clear that she knows what Bertha is up to.

BERTHA
But the ones who kept their babies...who wouldn't give them up...Didn't he ever let them back?

MRS CROFT
There was one time… but… that was because her baby died…

But Mrs Croft has said enough. With a sigh, she stands. It is the beginning of a new working day.

MRS CROFT (CONT'D)
Come on. Enough of this gabbing. Let's get started.

She moves away from her desk, revealing once more the poignant little tinted photograph of the long-dead, unforgotten infant.

131 INT. JENNINGS'S ROOM. DAY.

Jennings is bringing his cellar list up to date. Dexter looks in.

131 CONTINUED:

DEXTER
We'll be in touch. From now on we'll be working from the station. See if we can't manage things better from there.

JENNINGS
What about the poison? Haven't you traced that, at least?

DEXTER
Hardly. This house is a poisoner's paradise. We found the stuff in practically every room. And unfortunately no one's got a police record. 'Cept you, of course.

He chuckles but Jennings freezes. His worst nightmares are made flesh.

JENNINGS
What do you intend to do about it?

Dexter is genuinely surprised. He'd only been joshing.

DEXTER
What? You mean – ? Nothing. What should we do?

JENNINGS
Nothing?

DEXTER
Nah. I had a brother who was a conscientious objector. He did a bit of time, too. Why? Don't they know? Haven't you told them?

Jennings just looks at him.

DEXTER (CONT'D)
I should forget about it. The war's over. And you're too old to fight in another one. Right. Better be off. 'Bye then, Mr Jennings.

He is gone. A huge, leaden weight slides off the butler's shoulders.

132 INT. UPSTAIRS HALL AND CORRIDOR. DAY.

George is carrying the Nesbitts' cases down the stairs. They follow, talking softly.

FREDDIE
You're a fool. Now what are we supposed to do?

MABEL
Oh Freddie. Do try not to be so frightened all the time.

They move off camera as Arthur, climbing the stairs, takes us up to Barnes who is carrying luggage down with Sarah. Behind them are the Merediths.

ANTHONY
I don't know... I got to the door of the library and then I just thought... what's the point...? The truth is, I've made rather a fool of myself.

LAVINIA
Maybe... but you're *my* fool.

She squeezes his arm as they turn into the entrance hall where Jennings is seeing out the Nesbitts and Weissman is on the telephone.

WEISSMAN
What do you mean the butler didn't do it? If he didn't do it, then who the hell did?

Jennings, both wounded and mortally offended by this, holds the door for Anthony and Lavinia as the servants take out their things.

WEISSMAN (CONT'D)
What? Are you sure? When? Check it and call me in London.

Absently, he gives a smile to Jennings but the butler only returns a hurt glare as Renee passes by.

133 INT. STOCKBRIDGE'S BEDROOM. DAY.

Renee enters. Raymond stands by the window. Louisa reads a newspaper. She looks up.

133 CONTINUED:

RENEE
Beg pardon, milady, but what am I to do about the packing?Only you said last night that you might be staying on for a while...

Louisa does not answer but instead looks enquiringly at Raymond.

RAYMOND
It's not *my* decision.

LOUISA
On the contrary. It is *entirely* your decision.

She holds his gaze. No arm wrestlers in a dock-side pub could be more absorbed in their contest of wills. It is Raymond's knuckles which hit the tables first.

RAYMOND
Very well.

LOUISA
Don't say it if you don't mean it.

RAYMOND
I do mean it...I won't mention the subject again.

His capitulation is clear: He has purchased a scandal-free zone at the cost of never challenging his wife again over the whole William question. She is content.

LOUISA
Then thank you, yes, do pack. I'll be leaving with his lordship after all.

134 INT. UPSTAIRS HALL AND CORRIDOR. DAY.

On the stairs, Jeremy and Rupert whisper behind Arthur who carries their cases.

JEREMY
Did you ask her?

RUPERT
Not quite

JEREMY
On reflection, I think it's just as well.
(MORE)

(CONTINUED)

134 CONTINUED:

JEREMY (CONT'D)
According to the servants' hall gossip, she doesn't get any of the capital until her mother dies and if that's true it's too long to wait. You can do better.

Rupert opens his mouth to answer but before he can, Isobel steps round the corner at the base of the staircase. She must have heard. She looks carefully at Rupert.

ISOBEL
Have you checked your room? You mustn't leave anything behind.

135 INT. ELSIE'S ATTIC ROOM. DAY.

Elsie lies stretched out on her bed, reading a film magazine. She is smoking. The door opens. It is Mrs Wilson. Elsie glances over and then back to her magazine.

MRS WILSON
You know smoking up here is strictly forbidden.

Elsie takes a long, deep drag on her cigarette and blows a smoke ring.

MRS WILSON (CONT'D)
The other guests aren't leaving by train so the luggage car can run you to the station. You'll find it outside the front.

ELSIE
And that's it?

MRS WILSON
Let us know where you would like your reference to be sent.

She is about to go as Elsie stands.

ELSIE
I didn't mean nothing to him, you know. It was never serious…

MRS WILSON
Does it matter?

136 EXT. GOSFORD PARK. DAY.

George and Arthur are loading the last things into Jeremy's roadster. Off screen, the two young men and Isobel loiter by the vehicle.

ISOBEL (VO)
No, I shouldn't think of it. I know how your father hates it when someone's been in the papers and I'm afraid I'm bound to be.

RUPERT (VO)
What about January? When things have cooled off a bit…

The footmen come round to open the doors making them visible.

ISOBEL
Let's play it by ear, shall we? Well, goodbye. And thank you so much for coming. I am sorry it's all been so… dramatic.

Before Rupert can answer, she has gone, across the gravel, towards the house.

JEREMY
That was pretty painless.

RUPERT
No it wasn't.

In answer to Jeremy's curious stare, Rupert follows Isobel with his eyes.

RUPERT (CONT'D)
Not for me, anyway.

Amazing as it would be to Isobel, Rupert is in love with her. But it will do no good for she will never believe him now. With a sigh, he climbs into the car and starts it up.

137 INT. HALL/EXT. GOSFORD PARK. DAY.

As Jennings waits by the door, Weissman and Ivor cross the hall, dressed for travel.

IVOR
Why? What's happened?

137 CONTINUED:

WEISSMAN

They've brought in Sidney Kent as the new President of the Studio. He likes the Chan series and he's over-ruled Sheehan. The deadline's been dropped and I can cast whomever I like. Panic over.

IVOR

Just like that? What a weird and savage world you live in.

They have come out through the front door. Henry is already in their car. Pip sits alone and unloved on the steps watching as, at the far side of the house, Elsie's case is being put into one of the estate vehicles. Mary is with her.

MARY

Good luck. Don't do anything I wouldn't do.

ELSIE

Well, at least I know now that gives me some room for manoevre.

To their surprise, Weissman hails her from across the forecourt.

WEISSMAN

Hey! You there! Where are you going?

ELSIE

To the station.

WEISSMAN

Do you want a ride to London?

When she compares the battered farm car to the gleaming lagonda, the choice is easy.

ELSIE

Sure. Why not?

With a laugh, she siezes her case and runs to the car. As she climbs in she is distracted for a moment. The head of the unloved Pip makes a brief appearance from the top of her hold-all. Firmly, she pushes him back and climbs into the car. Ivor turns to see a look of disapproval on Jennings's face, though he can't know if he saw the dog. Maybe he did.

IVOR

I know, Jennings… but doesn't every creature deserve a second chance?

(CONTINUED)

137 CONTINUED: (2)

With a wave, he too climbs in and the vehicle moves off.

138 INT. TRENTHAM BEDROOM. DAY.

Mary is putting the last things in the suitcase, each carefully encased in a layer of tissue paper with crushed tissue to ease the folds. Constance is in travelling clothes. She addresses two envelopes, seals them and leaves them on the dressing-table.

CONSTANCE
Honestly, it's getting so expensive. By the time one does Jennings, *and* leaves something for the housemaids, one might as well have taken a suite at the Ritz. Tell me, what happened to William's little maid. I never saw her again after that dinner.

MARY
She's gone.

CONSTANCE
Pity really. I should have thought it was a good idea to have someone in the house who's actually sorry he's dead.

Sylvia looks round the door. If she heard she doesn't show it. Or, possibly, care.

CONSTANCE (CONT'D)
There you are, dear. Did you have a nice ride?

SYLVIA
I feel rather guilty. Apparently they've all gone. Except for you and Louisa... but there's no hurry. Why not stay for luncheon?

CONSTANCE
I'd better be off. Leave you in peace...

Sylvia, once more in jodphurs, sits on the bed near where Mary is packing, idly fingering a garment that is waiting to go in the case. Constance is applying lipstick.

CONSTANCE (CONT'D)
Now you will telephone with the funeral plans?

SYLVIA
You don't have to come if it's a bore.

(CONTINUED)

CONSTANCE
Nonsense. Of course I'm coming… Have you decided what you're going to do?

SYLVIA
Not really. I thought I might travel for a bit… Amelia Northbrook rang up this morning. They've taken a house in Alexandria for the winter and she's given me an open invitation…

CONSTANCE
That sounds lovely… and what about Gosford?

Sylvia shrugs, holding a scarf against herself to test the colour.

SYLVIA
I don't know… William loved it, of course. Fiddling with his guns… Tramping over his acres… not killing his pheasants… Poor William…

She finds another scarf better suited to her colouring. Constance nods, carefully patting her lipstick dry with a handkerchief she keeps for that purpose.

CONSTANCE
Yes. Poor, dear William. We shall miss him… So will you keep the place going, then?

SYLVIA
It's so difficult… I mean, these days, does one want the bother? It's not a family house, after all. Just bought with William's ill-gotten gains. I suppose I could shut it up for now and then make a decision when my head stops spinning.

CONSTANCE
Mrs Wilson can manage things until you're ready.

SYLVIA
Oh yes, *she* could manage things. Let's not worry about *that*… No doubt she'll sieze the chance to get rid of the wretched Mrs Croft.

138 CONTINUED: (2)

CONSTANCE
Why are they such enemies?

SYLVIA
Who knows? Something to do with when they were both in one of William's sweat shops. Mrs Croft was the senior then. She was a cook when Mrs Wilson was a lowly factory worker. Now she's gone up in the world and Mrs Croft can't adjust. Usual rubbish...

CONSTANCE
Was there ever a *Mister* Wilson? I Can't imagine it.

SYLVIA
Nor me. Although, funnily enough, I think there must have been.

CONSTANCE
Really? You amaze me.

SYLVIA
Well, unless she just changed her name...I know she had a different one when she first worked for William. Parker or Parkis or something.

A missing piece has fallen into place for Mary. She shuts the case and stands.

MARY
I'll go down and fetch the jewels.

CONSTANCE
Tell Merriman to come and get the bags.

139 INT. MRS WILSON'S ROOM. DAY.

Mrs Wilson is making notes in a linen book. She puts down her pen.

MARY
You're busy.

MRS WILSON
No, no. I was just checking the linen rotation. If I left it to the maids, the same twenty sheets would be used until they fell into rags...

(CONTINUED)

139 CONTINUED:

She smiles her professional smile as she waits for what Mary has to say.

MARY
Why did you do it?

Mrs Wilson stands and strolls over to the window, watching the activity outside.

MARY (CONT'D)
How did you know it was him? Was it the name? Or did you see the photograph in his room?

MRS WILSON
Ah. The photograph… What a miracle it survived...His mother put it in his blanket...She just wanted to feel he had something of hers, I suppose...What does he think happened to her?

MARY
They said she died. Just after he was born.

MRS WILSON
Well she didn't die. She gave him up. He promised the boy would be adopted. Said he knew the family. Turns out we all clung to that dream - all us girls. A better chance in life for our children and all the time he was dumping them - *his children* - in some godforsaken place - and I believed him. Maybe it was easier that way. My sister has always hated me for it.

MARY
Your sister?

MRS WILSON
Mrs Croft. Didn't you know? She kept hers - not many did, and it was very hard for her. She lost her job and then he died anyway - Scarlet Fever.

MARY
But how did you know Robert meant to harm his father?

Mrs Wilson looks at her for a moment.

139 CONTINUED: (2)

MRS WILSON
What gift do you think a good servant has that marks them apart from the rest? It is the gift of anticipation. And I am a good servant. I am better than good, I am the best, the *perfect* servant. I know when they are hungry so the food is waiting. I know when they will be tired so the bed is made and warmed. I know before they know it themselves.

MARY
Will you ever tell him?

MRS WILSON
Why would I? What purpose could it possibly serve?

MARY
What if they find out?

MRS WILSON
It's not a crime to stab a dead man. They can never touch him. That's what's important now, his life.

MARY
And your life? Isn't that important?

MRS WILSON
What do you mean? Didn't you hear me? I'm the Perfect Servant. I have no life.

There's a slight knock and George's head appears. He speaks to Mary.

GEORGE
Her ladyship's leaving now, miss.

MRS WILSON
Thank you, George. You should go now, Miss Trentham.

140 EXT. GOSFORD PARK. DAY.

In the foreground, Robert and a chauffeur are strapping luggage to the rack at the rear of a car. Raymond and Louisa stand with Sylvia. The sisters are quite cool.

(CONTINUED)

140 CONTINUED:

LOUISA (VO)
Well, goodbye. Let us know if there's anything we can do.

SYLVIA
Are you going away at all?

LOUISA
Not once the shooting's finished. I think we'll just put our feet up. Won't we, Raymond?

She glances at her husband. She is prepared to live in peace if he is.

Nearby stands Constance's car. Merriman puts in the luggage. Mary comes out, with dressing case and valise, as the Stockbridges get in. Robert strolls over as Renee tucks in Louisa and climbs into the front seat. The rear dicky is waiting for Robert.

MARY
Goodbye then.

ROBERT
Goodbye.

She hesitates, trying to think of what to say, but he touches her cheek.

ROBERT (CONT'D)
It's all right… It's over. It's finished.

Raymond opens his car door impatiently.

RAYMOND
Parks, for heaven's sake, can we get started?

With a smile, Robert crosses to the car, jumps in and they are away with Sylvia waving them off. As Mary walks over to give Merriman her valise, she sees Mrs Wilson's face, pressed against the basement window watching the dark head in the dicky as it moves off down the drive. Merriman takes the case and straps it on.

MERRIMAN
Crikey. Well. We've got something to write home about.

Constance, in travelling clothes, emerges from the front door.

140 CONTINUED: (2)

CONSTANCE
I've signed the book, though some of the others seem to have missed it. Goodbye dear. Chin up.

She kisses her niece and climbs into the car. Mary leans in and straightens the rug on Constance's knees, finds the basket with the thermos and sandwich box and places it nearby. Clearly while, in one way, everything has changed, in another, nothing has.

Mary climbs in and with a wave to Sylvia, the car moves off.

CONSTANCE (CONT'D)
Heavens, what a relief to be going. It'll take me a month to recover.

141 INT. DOWNSTAIRS HALL. DAY.

Mrs Wilson is on her way past the servants' hall when she catches sight of Dorothy.

DOROTHY
Have they gone?

MRS WILSON
Yes. I'll ask her ladyship if we're to lay luncheon in the dining-room. She may want a tray upstairs.

Dorothy nods but Mrs Wilson hasn't quite finished. She lowers her voice.

MRS WILSON (CONT'D)
Thank you for your help last night, Dorothy.

DOROTHY
You don't have to thank me. You know I'd kill for him if I had to.

Mrs Wilson goes into her room and Dorothy leaves. As she does, Mrs Croft emerges from the kitchen. Something draws her to the now closed door of Mrs Wilson's room. There is a sound of muffled weeping. She opens the door and goes in.

141A INT. MRS. WILSON'S ROOM. DAY.

Mrs Wilson is on the bed, wracked with sobbing, tears pouring down her cheeks.

(CONTINUED)

141A CONTINUED:

MRS CROFT
Don't cry, Jane, they'll hear you.

Mrs Wilson attempts to smother the noise but cannot stop. Mrs Croft crosses towards her.

MRS CROFT
Come on. You did what you thought was best for him at the time. I see that now.

She has joined the other woman on the bed.

MRS WILSON
I've lost him, Lizzie. I've lost him. He'll never know me. Never.

Mrs Croft takes her sister into her arms.

MRS CROFT
At least he's alive. That's what matters. At least your boy's alive...

And, after all, there is some comfort in this.

142 INT. CONSTANCE'S CAR. DAY.

Constance has relaxed a little. She winds down the window that divides her own seat from the two servants and speaks to the maid.

CONSTANCE
Mary, do you suppose, if there's a trial, I'd have to testify? Or you? I do hope not. I can't think of anything worse. Imagine a man being hanged because of something one said in a courtroom…

Mary looks at the countryside flashing by, thinking for a moment.

MARY
I know… and what purpose could it possibly serve?

Constance looks at her maid curiously for a moment before she winds up the window.

As the final credits roll, Constance picks up the thermos from the seat beside her and feebly tries to open it. Once again, she fails and reaches for the speaking tube.

(CONTINUED)

142 CONTINUED:

But this time, instead, she replaces the tube and tries the top of the thermos again. With the tiniest bit of effort she opens it, pours herself a drink and, with something like a sense of achievement, she sits back. Perhaps things have altered, after all. Just a little.

143 THE END

# STILLS

At the piano: Morris Weissman (*Bob Balaban*) and Ivor Novello (*Jeremy Northam)* with, foreground, Anthony Meredith (*Tom Hollander*) and Jennings (*Alan Bates*). Background: Lavinia Meredith (*Natasha Wightman*) and Sylvia McCordle (*Kristin Scott Thomas*).

In the kitchen, foreground: Bertha (*Teresa Churcher*), Mrs. Croft (*Eileen Atkins*), Henry Denton (*Ryan Phillippe*), and Mrs. Wilson (*Helen Mirren*).

Guests arrive at *Gosford Park*.

Constance (*Maggie Smith*) is attended to by her maid, Mary (*Kelly Macdonald*).

William McCordle (*Michael Gambon*) and Louisa Stockbridge (*Geraldine Somerville*)

In the Servants' Hall: foreground, George, the First Footman (*Richard E. Grant*) with Jennings, the Butler (*Alan Bates*).

Constance (*Maggie Smith*), Lavinia (*Natasha Wightman*), Anthony (*Tom Hollander),* Louisa (*Geraldine Somerville*), and Mabel Nesbitt (*Claudie Blakley*)

Ivor (*Jeremy Northam*), Morris (*Bob Balaban*), and Henry (*Ryan Phillippe*)

Mrs. Croft (*Eileen Atkins*) and Bertha (*Teresa Churcher*) count the knives, as Albert (*Will Beer*) walks by.

Dinner above stairs: Elsie (*Emily Watson*) serves in the dining room.

Dinner below stairs: Henry (*Ryan Phillippe*), Dorothy (*Sophie Thompson*), Barnes (*Adrian Scarborough*), May (*Emma Buckley*), Elsie (*Emily Watson*), and Robert (*Clive Owen*) in the Servants' Hall.

Robert Parks (*Clive Owen*)

Mabel (*Claudie Blakley*) and Ivor (*Jeremy Northam*) at the piano as Ivor sings "*I Can Give You the Starlight*"

Listening to the music below-stairs: Dorothy (*Sophie Thompson*), Fred (*Gregor Henderson Begg*), Ellen (*Sarah Flind*), and Albert (*Will Beer*)

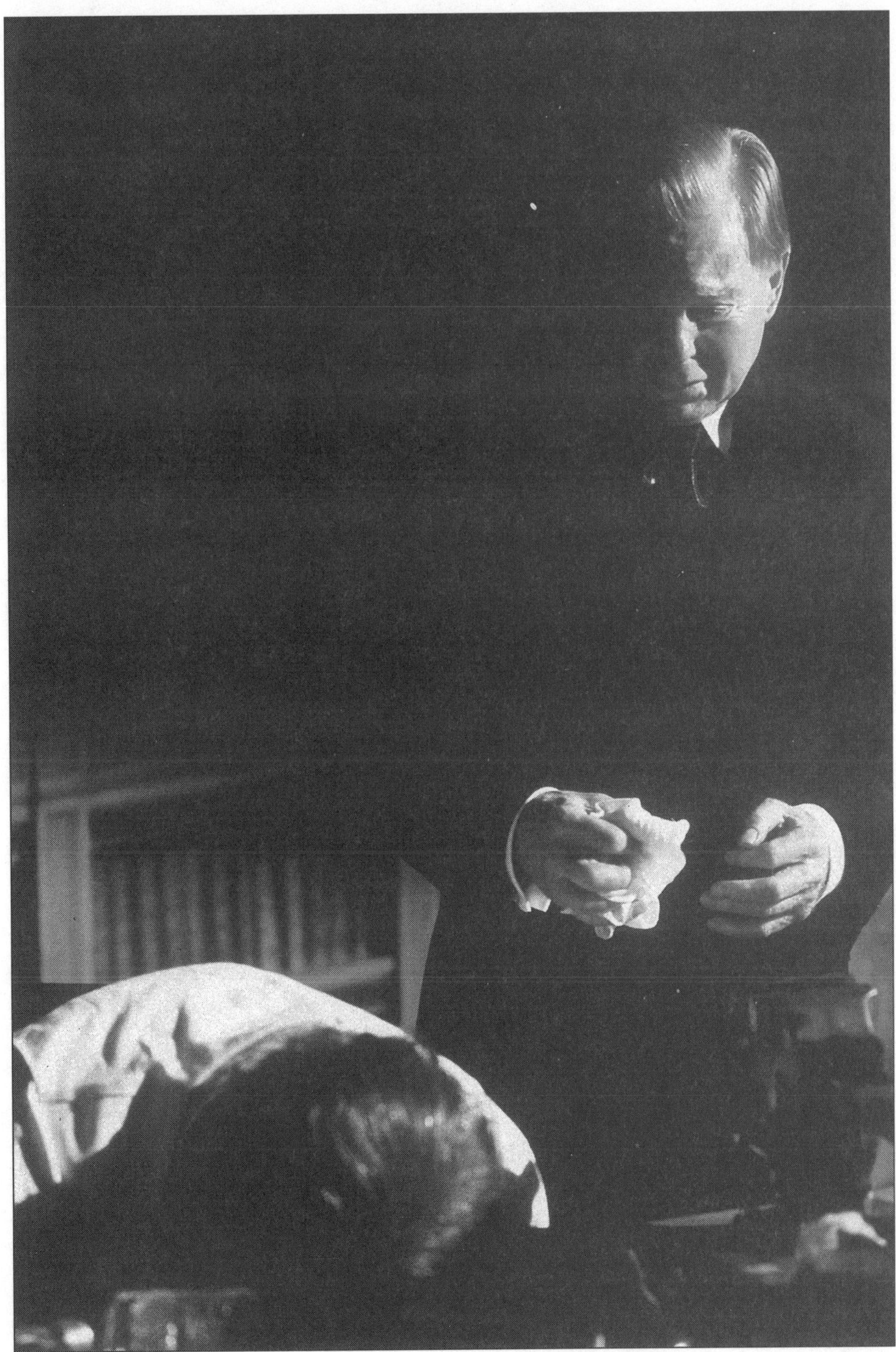

Probert (*Derek Jacobi*) in grief over William's corpse (*Michael Gambon*)

Henry Denton (*Ryan Phillippe)* and Sylvia (*Kristin Scott Thomas*)

Arthur (*Jeremy Swift*), Mrs. Wilson (*Helen Mirren*), and Inspector Thompson (*Stephen Fry*) in the Servants' Hall, with, seated, Sarah (*Frances Low*), Renee (*Joanna Maud*), and Barnes (*Adrian Scarborough*)

Robert (*Clive Owen*) and Mary (*Kelly Macdonald*)

Director Robert Altman

# BY JULIAN FELLOWES

Quite out of the blue, one January day in the year 2000, in the kitchen of my home in Chelsea, London, I received the telephone call that changed my life and stirred *Gosford Park* into existence. The actor/producer, Bob Balaban, for whom I had been working on another script, had suggested to Robert Altman that I might be the man to write his next project which was to be set, and made, in England. The idea was to examine the relationships between the classes in the context of a party at a large country house and, for good measure, in order to pay homage to the Agatha Christie tradition, one of the characters was to be "murdered twice." Twice? Yes, twice. Did I think I would be interested?

I did.

Of course I rushed out at once to find as many Altman videos as I could (some I already knew), and from this I soon realised that the film would be one of interweaving characters and plots, the more the merrier. Accordingly, I set about assembling a list of characters and their stories. Originally, Robert Altman had envisaged three distinct groups: The family, their guests, and their servants. But, at that time and in that class, people travelled with their own maids and valets, so I was able to add a fourth group to the mix. There would be visitors below stairs, as well as above, and they would prove useful in several story-lines. From the start, it was not Altman's intention that the murder plot should ever dominate the movie—either before or after it has taken place. "This isn't a Who-Dunnit," he declared. "It's a Who-Cares-Who-Dunnit." The film firmly places the emphasis on the characters, both principal and minor (in fact, in a very real way, there are no minor characters), each of whom would therefore need a complete arc—if not necessarily a finished story-line.

For the "spinal" (although I would not say "main") plot, it felt right to involve characters from both upstairs and down. I was reminded of the scandal of a millionaire shop-owner, William Whiteley, which I remembered hearing an aunt discussing when I was young. According to her version of the legend, Whiteley used his female employees much as William McCordle is reputed to have used his. These wretched girls were fired if they became pregnant and many fell into lives of prostitution and despair. Many years later, Whiteley was told there was a young man waiting to see him in his vast emporium not far from Kensington Palace. He went downstairs. His visitor informed him that he was in fact Whiteley's illegitimate son, the child of one of his miserable cast-offs, and stabbed him to death on the spot. It seemed to me that in these (possibly apocryphal) events there might be the roots of a tale that could link the two worlds of *Gosford Park*.

Many of the characters had their origins in my own life. My grandfather's eldest sister, one Mrs. Hamilton Stephenson, was the model for Constance Trentham. She was not a countess but her husband's sister was—the Countess of Clanwilliam. My aunt detested Lady Clanwilliam (rightly or wrongly, I know not) and railed against her sister-in-law for all the years I knew her. I was always amused to hear her as every quality that my aunt objected to in Lady C., she shared. It was this total lack of self-knowledge that formed her armour and repelled all comers and that, I felt, should be the core quality of Lady Trentham. She would represent those aristocrats who are impervious and even hostile to change. So, on her first arrival, irritated by the wretched Mabel's awe in the presence of the Matinée Idol, Ivor Novello, Constance deliberately makes it clear that she despises Novello's world and his work: "It must be so disappointing when something just *flops* like that," she sneers. Later, in one of the movie's most memorable moments, she will dismiss the latest effort of the film-maker, Weissman, with: "None of us will ever see it." She must demonstrate that the values of these outsiders hold no interest for her—just as she is unflinchingly hostile to William, despite needing his money, and indeed to anyone who is not drawn from her own background.

However, we wanted to avoid the cliché of characters whom the audience is instructed to dislike and because I needed one relationship to show the intimacy and near-friendship that was a frequent feature of the mistress-and-maid situation, it seemed right that she, Constance, should be the on-screen example of this. Her scenes with her maid, Mary, are the most relaxed examples of inter-class gossip in the film. Because Mary does not challenge, but rather endorses, Constance's class-based philosophies, there is no antagonism between them. Incidentally, one feature of this pseudo-friendship was always that it could only be maintained in a one-to-one situation without witnesses. So, Constance and Mary are chatting about the incident at the shooting luncheon; however, when Sylvia enters the room, immediately she and Constance become the talkers, and Mary reverts to the role of non-person without needing to be instructed to do so.

The names came largely from my past or present. "Constance" was taken partly from my cousin, Constance Lloyd, Mrs. Oscar Wilde, and partly used because it amused me to name Lady Trentham, that least generous of women, after one of the virtues. "McCordle" I simply saw in a book and liked, but "Sylvia" was called after a friend of my mother's as I have always found it a haunting name. "Louisa" had two parents, Lady Portal and Lady Louisa Uloth, both current friends, and "Lavinia" was borrowed from a pal of my early years in the theatre, Lavinia Dyer. And so on. I have always found that certain names, once heard, seem to strike some inner bell and linger on, faintly, in the back of my mind until there is an excuse to use them. Stockbridge is a town near where my wife grew up and, most important of all, the house (and, once Bob had decided on it, the film) is named after an old and dear family friend, Francesca, Countess of Gosford, who happened to announce that she was emigrating to join her daughter in America the very week I was given the commission. "You'll forget all about me," she said. "On the contrary," I replied, "I'll make your name famous." I am happy to report that Lady Gosford attended the première in Los Angeles.

In early drafts Sylvia and Louisa were siblings and Lavinia was simply a friend until Bob decided that the symmetry of the piece would be better served if they were Three Sisters. I agreed not least because this underpinned the entire Anthony/McCordle story and made it far more plausible. The marriages of the sisters, Sylvia, Louisa and Lavinia, were designed to illustrate different aspects of the aristocratic dilemma of how to marry satisfactorily and yet maintain caste. While the English upper classes will always tell you they never talk about money, the truth is they think of nothing else. The poor aristocrat, both in fiction and in life, is an absurdity, a figure of fun. So here we have the three daughters of an impoverished earl trying to survive. We are told, through servants' gossip confirmed by Constance, that the rich *parvenu* William McCordle wanted to marry a noblewoman and would have taken either of the two eldest, while their father, Lord Carton, didn't care which of them married him as long as one of them did. It was Robert Altman who suggested they had cut cards to decide. Unfortunately, in the intervening years, Sylvia has come to find William's vulgarity unacceptable while Louisa, who has married the rich but stolid Lord Stockbridge, yearns for a man with vigour who is not encased in the prejudices of his class, who doesn't only feel comfortable "with his own kind" as she complains to William in the library. I must say at once that I do not agree with Louisa's assessment of her husband. Largely because Charles Dance, with enormous subtlety and minimal dialogue in one of my favourite performances of the film, manages to define Stockbridge as a poignant figure, decent and lonely, who is imprisoned by his inability to communicate with his wife.

At any rate, by November 1932, each sister has come to believe she would be happier with the other's husband. Lavinia, on the other hand, has married Anthony Meredith, with whom she is perfectly happy but who is an abject failure in business. The point being made with them is that, in this world, poverty and failure are the great crimes that obliterate all virtue. Even though the Merediths are the only well-suited and happy couple, they are universally despised within the family. It will take a servant, who is not pre-conditioned by these values, to show Anthony that he is in possession of the one gift of lasting value—a strong and loving relationship.

The theme of money as the life-blood of aristocracy is continued in the story of the Nesbitts. Freddie is the feckless son of a peer who has married the middle-class daughter of a glove manufacturer for her money. She is flattened by the life he has brought her into, oppressed by her constant sense of inadequacy. We are given the first glimpse of Mabel as someone who is more than her husband realises when we see how she can respond to the culture of the day, represented here by Novello (for more on which see page 171), and during the course of the movie she starts to see her husband for what he is—a scared and pathetic man. We have (at least I hope we have) a sense that, after this particular house-party she will never allow herself to be bullied again. "Oh Freddie," she says as they descend the stairs, "do try not to be so *frightened* all the time."

Obviously, with all these story-lines, the writing had to be extremely economical, and I was vastly helped by Robert Altman's belief that an audience has to pay attention and not be spoon fed all the information. It is customary these days to give the salient plot facts about fifty times during the course of the film but, clearly, there was no time for that here. Most of the information is given, or only suggested, once or twice. For example, we know, within the film's narrative, that Sylvia has chosen to slake her lust with a handsome servant. What we do not know at first is that this is her habit. It satisfies her without confusing the life she has made for herself. Only two lines tells us it is a regular event and that the household knows: The first is after she has visited the Servants' Hall and has set eyes on the handsome valet, Henry Denton. When she leaves, George, the footman, looks over at Denton. "You're all set, then," he says. Later, after Denton has been exposed as a fraud, and we know Sylvia is going to have the embarrassment of sitting in the drawing-room with him in front of the others, it is the cook, Mrs. Croft, who remarks that the "joke" is "on Lady Sylvia." In the original script, this line belonged to Bertha, the kitchen maid, but it means more coming from an authority figure in the house. At any rate, these are the only two lines which tell us the servants know all about it. Miss them and you miss that plot point.

Another of Robert Altman's script philosophies that was music to my ears was his conviction that not everything has to be resolved to the last detail. An example would be the Jennings/Dorothy relationship. I am always interested in the whole business of unrequited love and whether it is more or less satisfactory than having no love at all. Another thing that fascinates me is the way we can, all of us, engender love or indeed hatred without being in the least aware of it. How suddenly one can realise that a person we had taken for an acquaintance is instead passionately involved with us in their own imagination. Since, once again, economy was all-important, the audience is given only a few moments to guess at Dorothy's love for Jennings—the Servants' Hall dinner where she supports his tyranny and her bleakness at his reprimand in the dining-room after the quarrel—but so superb are the performances of both Alan Bates and Sophie Thompson that I am confident that when Dorothy offers to lie to the police we are not surprised. Instead, we can enjoy Jennings's horror at the level of emotion he has unconsciously aroused. However, as far as a final resolution is concerned, there is none. Recently, I was asked: "Does Dorothy know Jennings's secret or does she just know he's *got* a secret?"

"I don't know," I replied. "What do you think?"

There are many stories within the film which are never quite buttoned up: Were William and Louisa lovers? Was Freddie the father of Isobel's aborted baby? Why does Barnes dislike his master so particularly? What happened in the past between Raymond and Sylvia? Why does Denton allow himself to be used by Weissman? There are others that are: Who is the baby in Mrs. Croft's photograph? Who is the woman in Robert's? What was going on between William and Elsie? But even in these, I hope there is a margin for the audience to be able to disagree about probable outcomes. It was Altman's, and my, intention that it should be so. My greatest pleasure is when I hear cinema-goers arguing over the significance of this detail or that line. Perhaps best of all, was one enthusiastic fan who queried me about Isobel's past. "Oh no," she said, when I had explained the story implied in those scenes. "I think you're quite wrong. I don't think that happened *at all*."

Downstairs, the servants fall roughly into two groups: Those who imagine this way of life is going to continue forever and those who sense that it is approaching the end. This quality of fragility, of it all beginning to break apart, was key in the initial brief. Bob wanted it to take place as late as possible before the end of this way of life. Of course fragments of it would continue to the present day but, as a nation-wide accepted manner of existence, it was finished by the Second World War so that meant the nineteen-thirties. I was certain that it had to be a shooting party as the rituals of shooting echo the rituals by which they lived their lives and sport was the *raison d'etre* of this existence so that tied us to the winter months. Bob didn't want Christmas imagery and neither of us wanted another film taking place under the shadow of Hitler. Since the Nazis burned down the *Reichstag* in January 1933, that meant that November 1932 was the last date which fulfilled all the qualifications.

In real life, within seven or eight years the younger servants, George, Arthur, the hallboys, and the grooms, would be called up. Later most of the younger women, Dorothy, Bertha, the kitchenmaids, and the housemaids, would follow them into war work. The next six years would give them a taste of living their own lives instead of someone else's and, as a result, when peace came in 1945, very few would want to return to the shackles of their previous servitude. At Gosford Park, we can easily see that George has had enough. Barnes is yearning to go and who could believe that Robert would come back to the life once he'd escaped? In a way, this approaching "break-out" is represented here by Elsie. When she climbs into Weissman's car at the end, we hope he will give her a part in his movie—perhaps that of the cockney maid that he has already discussed on the telephone. However, be that as it may, one thing we the audience do, or should, know is that Elsie is *never* going back into service. That part of her life is over as it would be for millions of her contemporaries barely eight years later.

Jennings, on the other hand, or Lewis, Lady Sylvia's maid, are content with, and on the whole unquestioning about, the hierarchy which may keep them below stairs but which nevertheless accords them status and privilege there. It has always seemed to me bogus to suggest that every servant was a pitiful and tormented creature, ruthlessly exploited by the moneyed classes.

Obviously, if this had been the case, the system would not have lasted for thousands of years and, indeed, would not be in place still in many parts of the world. The servants had to be complicit for it all to work, and it is true that the rules of precedence and rank were as rigidly enforced below stairs as above—if anything, more so. I was keen to show how even the re-naming of servants was endorsed by their fellows. We hear Robert dismiss Lord Stockbridge with the words: "He thinks he's God Almighty but they all do." But we later see him reverentially tying Charles Dance's dressing gown cord as if he *were* God Almighty. The truth is, in many ways, they were all in it together.

Robert Altman is especially keen, when dealing with a period subject, that one should never lose the sense that these were real people leading real lives. I remember his discussion with Jenny Beavan, the designer: "I want clothes," he said, "not costumes." Obviously, this applies to the dialogue. You don't want it to have a modern sound which would jar but, at the same time, you must avoid period-speak. To this end, I attempted to keep the rhythms fairly colloquial but to employ phrases that suggested a time slightly before our own. This was particularly true of Constance: "I call that very feeble," "it's hard to know when it's time to throw in the towel," "we all have to pull our weight," and "she's not all mean in *that* way." I remember these words, or something similar, in the mouths of my grandmother and great aunts, all of whom were born between 1880 and 1895, making them a little younger than Constance and a little older than Sylvia and Louisa. Throughout the script, I tried to drop in expressions, "I'm making bricks without straw," "I'll be wide awake and bored to sobs," "I think it's too clever for any words," "charging into the cannon's mouth," and "one might as well take a suite at the Ritz," which lightly suggest another time, another place, without seeming to drag you there.

Aristocratic anti-Semitism was widely in evidence in the years before the war. It still exists but to a lesser extent as the horrors of Nazi rule diminished it—even if it is not expunged altogether. There is no doubt that an unwillingness to sympathise with the Jews, a willing, self-imposed blindness in fact, among the establishment at that time, protected Hitler and his régime for years. What was particularly insidious about this was that it did not, for the most part, consist of overt, violent hatred, simply a dismissive, patronising distancing of society from the Jew. I had always wanted one member of the party to be a total outsider—not a semi-outsider like William or Mabel who have, to a degree, learned the rules but someone from another planet. Because of the theme of popular culture versus the aristocracy, it felt right for this outsider to be a film-maker from Hollywood. By making him Jewish, which many of the first producers were, it would be possible to introduce a faint strain of anti-Semitism into *Gosford Park*. Deliberately, this is implied rather than under-scored. Lady Trentham's recoiling from Weissman's greeting on the road: "Are you OK?" "Am I *what*?"; Lord Stockbridge's awkward reception of Weissman's name; Sylvia's dismissal of him to Thompson; and Louisa's patronising, "Who's the funny little American?" Nobody befriends him. Nobody warms to him. Throughout the film, Weissman is treated by the others with a kind of cold indifference. They are not quite rude but never welcoming, a fore-runner of the cold indifference that would greet the stories coming out of Nazi Germany.

Incidentally, it was after I had included Weissman, the producer among the guests, that Bob came up with the idea that he was about to make *Charlie Chan in London*, a real if totally forgotten film starring Warner Olund which came out in 1933. Apart from providing "Raymond" Milland with his acting début, there is nothing remarkable about it. Even so when, miraculously, I discovered a copy in the library of a friend of mine in Florida, we had a lot of fun watching it.

After completing the first draft, I flew out to Los Angeles to spend a few days with Bob Altman and go through it. This was the moment when he suggested that Ivor Novello might be included as one of the guests. Bob was already familiar with Novello's charming and rather forgotten music, and he felt that a real-life character would fasten the film into its own period. I agreed completely. Not least because it gave a far more convincing reason for Weissman to be there (I think, originally, I had him as an acquaintance of William's which was less convincing), but also it allowed the film to explore two more themes. Bob thought Ivor might perhaps be a cousin of Sylvia's to make it plausible that he is there at all. He could not, in fact, be a cousin of Sylvia's as he was the lower-middle class son of a Welsh music teacher, but he could certainly have been a cousin of the *nouveau riche* William. Despite this, despite clearly getting on quite well with Sylvia and Louisa, Ivor's character allows us to make the point that, with these people, however intimate you are with them, you are never really a part of their world unless you are born into it. There is a distance that separates, and Ivor can only ever aspire to be there as an entertainer—which he knows. In our film he has bargained his piano skills, so useful for enlivening the party, to get an invitation for his Hollywood friend. Like the older servants below, he does not challenge the inequities of the system but, in Jeremy Northam's wonderfully wise and melancholy performance, it is clear he is aware of them. "How do you manage these people?" Weissman asks. Ivor wearily replies, "You forget. I make my living impersonating them."

But the second theme that Ivor enabled is central to the film. In retrospect, one of the signs that the upper classes were losing their grip on public life in Britain between the wars was that they started to lose any connection with the popular culture of the day. In the nineteenth century when the theatre and opera had provided the great stars of the day, the aristocracy had been a willing audience and enthusiastic patrons. But the twentieth century started to throw up forms, moving pictures, and popular music, which seemed to have more connection with the working man than with them. In a way, film is the first major art form to evolve originally as a working class pastime. Eventually, the upper classes, or sections of them, would retreat into a kind of tweed-wearing, television-eschewing bunker by no means vanished today, but even then, when they still occupied high office, there were signs that the twentieth century was getting away from them. To illustrate this, Robert Altman mounts what is to me one of the most brilliant sequences in the movie.

There has been an uncomfortable dinner, McCordle has flounced out, and Sylvia, showing Ivor precisely what his function is, makes her request: "Is it too awful to ask you to play something? And brighten things up a bit?" So he starts to play. Almost immediately Constance makes it clear that this music is beneath her and, more tellingly, actually prevents the young people at her bridge table from enjoying it. Before long, Sylvia and Louisa are chatting, Raymond is writing... Of all the company in the drawing-room only Mabel, the one woman there who is not conditioned by an aristocratic upbringing, is able to have a fresh and unfeigned response to the tunes. For the first time we see that she is more than a down-trodden rag. At the same time, the servants gradually gather to listen, in the hall, below stairs, hidden in the various doorways and corridors. What is clear is that they are possessed of a kind of energy, an enthusiasm for sensation, while their employers are jaded and unable to accommodate the new. In other words, the lower classes are looking forward to the future, which will be their time; the upper classes, on the other hand, are looking forward only to the past. All this is achieved with very little dialogue but with a series of visual images, haunting and beautiful as well as bitter and funny. By the time the music stops, Altman has given you information about every person there.

Originally, when the time came for the introduction of the police, I had thought to play them very much in the background. They would be hardly glimpsed and instead all the information would reach us, as so much does throughout the film, through servants' gossip. However, Bob felt this was a mistake. He believed that in order to persuade the audience that they didn't have to take the murder seriously or concentrate especially on the suspects, it was necessary to make the inspector actually comedic. Accordingly, I returned to the drawing-board and Inspector Thompson was born. It meant a strange change of tempo two-thirds of the way through the movie, and I was nervous as to whether or not the audiences would be prepared to follow us there, but the proof of the pudding is in the eating and, when the film reached the public, it was clear I had been wrong. They were content to laugh at Stephen Fry, to be relieved of the burden of having to be concerned about the murder, and were perfectly willing to return to the original pace of the story as soon as he had departed. The smoothness of the manner in which this was handled by Bob and by his brilliant Director of Photography, Andrew Dunn, is the main reason, I think anyway, why the transition does not jar. Just as the mobile, seductive camera that prowls the house throughout allows us to swim upstairs and downstairs and, literally, into My Lady's Chamber without any feeling of being jerked around.

Robert Altman's skill in visual narrative is extraordinary. He is a genius. And I speak as one who stood and watched for nearly three months as impossible shot after impossible shot was achieved. It would have been out of the question for most directors to tackle a subject with this many stories and this many characters but, somehow, Altman manages to make it all work by knowing precisely at what point his camera will be gliding past which action. Even now I cannot imagine how. I remember, very early on, we were shooting the scene in Lady Trentham's bedroom when they are all getting ready to go to the shooting luncheon. The actresses were rattling through their lines, everything seemed to be happening at once, and the cameras were wheeling here, there, and everywhere. And I was in a panic. There were several important points to be made for different stories: Lavinia's money troubles, Sylvia's disappointment in her own daughter, the house party's contempt for Mabel, as well as some lines that I thought were worth keeping: "There's no point in looking at me. If I open my mouth on the subject, it'll only make it worse." "What *are* you wearing?" "Why? Don't you like it? You bought it." "Did I? How extraordinary of me." Or, one of my own favourites from Constance, "Me? I haven't a snobbish bone in my body." How any, never mind all, of this was going to survive the chaotic talk soup I saw being enacted was beyond me. The following day, I filed into the dailies with a sinking heart. I should have had more faith. Every plot point, every line, was as clear as a bell. Miraculously, the camera was invariably and precisely where you wanted it to be. This is the brilliance of a genuinely imaginative mind, Robert Altman's amazing gift.

My extraordinary privilege throughout this period was to be on the set every day, for every shot. It is a courtesy seldom extended to the authors of screenplays. This was partly in my capacity as "technical adviser" where the details of the lives of these people were concerned, but it also afforded me the opportunity to re-write when necessary, to move information if a scene had been cut, and to rescue a discarded line and re-locate it. Constance's remark about Mabel "travelling light" was one example of this. Maggie Smith and I both liked it so when it was dropped from Scene 64 we found another home for it later in the film. Obviously the basic stories were settled before we started shooting, but I was there if any details needed adjustment. One day, during lunch, about two weeks into filming, Bob asked me if I noticed anything about Eileen and Helen, now that they were in their make-up and costumes. I looked and realised with a start what Bob had seen. The two actresses were astonishingly like one another. "Let's make 'em sisters," said Bob. That afternoon I was writing the sister plot. I was even on hand if brand new dialogue was suddenly required. When Bob decided that he wanted to see the Stockbridges come down to tea and Geraldine appealed for help, I remembered a remark I'd heard at a Norfolk shooting party when a husband had been complaining to his wife that the other guests were uncomfortably "arty." I slightly re-phrased her answer for Louisa: "It's a relief to me to sit next to someone who isn't deaf in one ear." All this, as most readers will know, constitutes an enormous bonus for any writer just as it testifies to a tremendous generosity on the part of the director. I am grateful for many, many aspects of this whole project but being made welcome throughout the filming was certainly among the major blessings.

As any Altman aficionado will know, there was some improvisation on the set, but those instances that made it into the final edit are not included in this published script excepting only in the reconciliation of Eileen Atkins and Helen Mirren. The decision was made on the day to shoot it and I wrote the scene but, in the event, apart from the opening line, "Don't cry, Jane, they'll hear you," it is substantially the work of those two great actresses.

Of course, the hardest moment for any writer is to see which scenes and which parts of scenes have been dropped in the final film (just as the best moment is when he sees his script being filmed at all). The reader of this book will learn of one whole plot (McCordle's will) that was excised, along with some favourite moments of mine. I still miss Probert's plans for his future, as well as the quarrels between the Stockbridges which were quite wonderfully acted by Charles Dance and Geraldine Somerville, and the last confrontation between Sylvia and Henry Denton: "I just don't see what's changed." "Then you are a fool as well as a liar." The truth is that a film has a certain rhythm and just because a scene is excellent it does not necessarily mean it will find a place in the finished product if it seems to impede the flow. The pace required of a movie watched at home, where it may be stopped and started at will, is slightly different, and there is a chance that some, if not all, of the absent moments may re-surface in the DVD version which I hope. Whether they do or not, I enjoy the thought of the reader seeing these moments denied to the cinema-goer.

At all events, *Gosford Park* has been the most significant adventure of my career so far. Of course having my first feature screenplay directed by Robert Altman with a cast that outshines MGM's famous boast of having "more stars than there are in heaven" does mean it will be difficult to equal in the coming years. I have started at the top which can be difficult to move on from. But even if I have few professional experiences to look forward to which will be as blessed as this one, I have at least known what it is to work with the very best this business has to offer.

USA FILMS presents in association with CAPITOL FILMS and the FILM COUNCIL
a SANDCASTLE 5 production in association with
CHICAGOFILMS and MEDUSA FILM

Eileen Atkins  Bob Balaban  Alan Bates  Charles Dance
Stephen Fry  Michael Gambon  Richard E. Grant  Tom Hollander
Derek Jacobi  Kelly Macdonald  Helen Mirren  Jeremy Northam  Clive Owen
Ryan Phillippe  Maggie Smith  Geraldine Somerville  Kristin Scott Thomas
Sophie Thompson  Emily Watson  James Wilby

# GOSFORD PARK

Casting
Mary Selway

Costumes
Jenny Beavan

Music
Patrick Doyle

Editor
Tim Squyres, A.C.E.

Production Design
Stephen Altman

Director of Photography
Andrew Dunn, B.S.C.

Co-Producers
Jane Frazer
Joshua Astrachan

Executive Producers
Jane Barclay
Sharon Harel
Robert Jones
Hannah Leader

Producers
Robert Altman
Bob Balaban
David Levy

Written by
Julian Fellowes

Based upon an idea by
Robert Altman
and Bob Balaban

Directed by
Robert Altman

Sir William McCordle . . . . . . . . . . . . Michael Gambon
Lady Sylvia McCordle . . . . . . . . . . Kristin Scott Thomas
Isobel McCordle . . . . . . . . . . . . . . Camilla Rutherford
Constance, Countess of Trentham . . . . . . . . Maggie Smith
Raymond, Lord Stockbridge . . . . . . . . . . Charles Dance
Louisa, Lady Stockbridge . . . . . . . . . Geraldine Somerville
Lieutenant Commander Anthony Meredith . . Tom Hollander
Lady Lavinia Meredith . . . . . . . . . . . Natasha Wightman
The Hon. Freddie Nesbitt . . . . . . . . . . . . . James Wilby
Mabel Nesbitt. . . . . . . . . . . . . . . . . Claudie Blakley
Lord Rupert Standish . . . . . . . . . . . . . . . Laurence Fox
Jeremy Blond. . . . . . . . . . . . . . . . . . . . . Trent Ford
Ivor Novello . . . . . . . . . . . . . . . . . Jeremy Northam
Morris Weissman. . . . . . . . . . . . . . . . . . Bob Balaban
Jennings . . . . . . . . . . . . . . . . . . . . . . Alan Bates
Mrs. Wilson . . . . . . . . . . . . . . . . . . . Helen Mirren
Mrs. Croft. . . . . . . . . . . . . . . . . . . . . Eileen Atkins
Probert. . . . . . . . . . . . . . . . . . . . . . . Derek Jacobi
Elsie. . . . . . . . . . . . . . . . . . . . . . . . Emily Watson
George . . . . . . . . . . . . . . . . . . . . Richard E. Grant
Arthur . . . . . . . . . . . . . . . . . . . . . . . Jeremy Swift
Lewis. . . . . . . . . . . . . . . . . . . . . Meg Wynn Owen
Dorothy . . . . . . . . . . . . . . . . . . . Sophie Thompson
Bertha . . . . . . . . . . . . . . . . . . . . . . Teresa Churcher
Ellen. . . . . . . . . . . . . . . . . . . . . . . . . . Sarah Flind
Lottie . . . . . . . . . . . . . . . . . . . . . . . . . Lucy Cohu
Janet . . . . . . . . . . . . . . . . . . . . . . . Finty Williams
May . . . . . . . . . . . . . . . . . . . . . . . . Emma Buckley
Ethel . . . . . . . . . . . . . . . . . . . . . . . . Laura Harling
Maud . . . . . . . . . . . . . . . . . . . . . . . . Tilly Gerrard
Albert . . . . . . . . . . . . . . . . . . . . . . . . . . Will Beer
Fred . . . . . . . . . . . . . . . . . . . Gregor Henderson Begg
Jim . . . . . . . . . . . . . . . . . . . . . . . . . . . . Leo Bill
Strutt . . . . . . . . . . . . . . . . . . . . . . . . Ron Puttock
McCordles' loader . . . . . . . . . . . . . . . . Adrian Preater
Mary Maceachran . . . . . . . . . . . . . . . Kelly Macdonald
Robert Parks . . . . . . . . . . . . . . . . . . . . . Clive Owen
Henry Denton. . . . . . . . . . . . . . . . . . . Ryan Phillippe
Renee . . . . . . . . . . . . . . . . . . . . . . . Joanna Maude
Barnes . . . . . . . . . . . . . . . . . . . . Adrian Scarborough
Sarah . . . . . . . . . . . . . . . . . . . . . . . . . Frances Low
Merriman . . . . . . . . . . . . . . . . . . . . . . John Atterbury
Burkett. . . . . . . . . . . . . . . . . . . . . . . Frank Thornton
Inspector Thompson . . . . . . . . . . . . . . . . . Stephen Fry
Constable Dexter . . . . . . . . . . . . . . . . . . Ron Webster

Loaders . . . . . . . . . . . . . . . . . . John Cox, Ken Davies,
Tony Davies, Steve Markham,
Terry Sturmey, Julian Such
Beaters . . . . . . . . . . . . . . Alan Bland, Peter Champion,
Geoff Double, Robin Devereux,
John Fountain, Richard Gamble,
Brian Rumsey, George Sherman

Directed by . . . . . . . . . . . . . . . . . . . Robert Altman
Written by . . . . . . . . . . . . . . . . . . . . Julian Fellowes
Based upon an idea by . . . . Robert Altman and Bob Balaban
Producers . . . . . . . . . . . . . . . . . . . . Robert Altman
Bob Balaban
David Levy
Executive Producers . . . . . . . . . . . . . . . . Jane Barclay
Sharon Harel
Robert Jones
Hannah Leader
Co-Producers . . . . . . . . . . . . . . . . . . . . Jane Frazer
Joshua Astrachan
Director of Photography . . . . . . . . Andrew Dunn, B.S.C.
Production Design . . . . . . . . . . . . . . . Stephen Altman
Editor . . . . . . . . . . . . . . . . . . . . Tim Squyres, A.C.E.
Music . . . . . . . . . . . . . . . . . . . . . . . . Patrick Doyle
Costumes . . . . . . . . . . . . . . . . . . . . . Jenny Beavan
Casting . . . . . . . . . . . . . . . . . . . . . . . Mary Selway

1st Assistant Director . . . . . . . . . . . . . . . Richard Styles

Production Manager . . . . . . . . . . . . . . . . . Tori Parry

Production Accountant . . . . . . . . . . . Alistair Thompson

Camera Operator . . . . . . . . . . . . . . . . . . Peter Taylor

Script Supervisor . . . . . . . . . . . . . . . . . . Penny Eyles

Chief Make-up Artist . . . . . . . . . . . . . . . . . Sallie Jaye

Hair Designer . . . . . . . . . . . . . . . . . . . Jan Archibald

Sound Mixer . . . . . . . . . . . . . . . . . . . Peter Glossop

Supervising Art Director . . . . . . . . . . . . . John Frankish

Set Decorator . . . . . . . . . . . . . . . . . . Anna Pinnock

Location Manager . . . . . . . . . . . . . . . . . . . Sue Quinn

Supervising Sound Editor . . . . . . . . Nigel Mills (M.P.S.E.)

Re-Recording Mixers . . . . . . . . . . . Robin O'Donoghue
Richard Street

Associate Producer . . . . . . . . . . . . . . . . Julian Fellowes

Production Coordinator . . . . . . . . . . . . Winnie Wishart
Assistant Production Coordinator . . . . . . . . . . Anya Keith
Director's Assistant . . . . . . . . . . . . . . . . . . May Chu
Producer's Assistant . . . . . . . . . . . . . . . . . . Brett Tyne
Production Runner . . . . . . . . . . . . . . . . Ben Rakison
Post-Production Assistant . . . . . . . . . . Sacha Guttenstein

U.S. Post-Production Assistant . . . . . . . . Lowell Dubrinksy

For Sandcastle 5 Productions . . . . . . . . . . . Wren Arthur
For Chicagofilms . . . . . . . . . . . . . . . . . . Allison Shigo

2nd Assistant Director . . . . . . . . . . . . . . Sara Desmond
3rd Assistant Director . . . . . . . . . . . . . . . . Carlos Fidel
Floor Runners . . . . . . . . . . . . . . . . . Caroline Chapman
Clare (Woody) Wade
Additional Floor Runners . . . . . . . . . . . . . . Vicki Allen
Samar Pollitt

Focus Pullers . . . . . . . . . . . . . . . . . . . . Brad Larner
Mikael Allen
Clapper Loaders . . . . . . . . . . . . . . . . . Paul Wheeldon
Richard Sion Carroll
Grips . . . . . . . . . . . . . . . . . . . . . . . . . Pat Garrett
Malcolm Huse
Video Operator . . . . . . . . . . . . . . . . . . Stephen Lee
Video Assistant . . . . . . . . . . . . . . . . . . . Derek Boyes
Camera Trainee . . . . . . . . . . . . . . . . Charlie Stanfield
Additional Focus Puller . . . . . . . . . . . . Eamon O'Keefe
Stills Photographer . . . . . . . . . . . . . . . . . . Mark Tillie

Boom Operators . . . . . . . . . . . . . . . . . . . Shaun Mills
Benjamin Bober
Sound Assistant . . . . . . . . . . . . . . . . . . Mark Gudgin

Casting Assistant . . . . . . . . . . . . . . . . . . . . Fiona Weir

1st Assistant Accountant . . . . . . . . . . . Claire Robertson
2nd Assistant Accountant . . . . . . . . . . . . . Julian Murray
Trainee Accounts Assistant . . . . . . . . . . . . . Zoie Miller

Unit Manager . . . . . . . . . . . . . . . . Joseph Jayawardena
Location Assistants . . . . . . . . . . . . . . . . . Simon August
Hamish Tavendale

Unit Publicist . . . . . . . . . . . . . . . . Claudia Kalindjian

1st Assistant Editor . . . . . . . . . . . . . . . Amanda Pollack
2nd Assistant Editor . . . . . . . . . . . . . . . . John F. Lyons
Editing Room Assistant . . . . . . . . . . . . . . . . Betty Teng
U.K. Assistant Editors . . . . . . . Emily Grant, Will MacNeil

Supervising Dialogue Editor . . . . . . . . . . Nina Hartstone
ADR Editor . . . . . . . . . . . . . . . . . . . . . Rob Ireland
Foley Editor . . . . . . . . . . . . . . . . . . . Grahame Peters
Dialogue Editors . . . . . . . . Howard Halsall, John Cochrane
Music Editor . . . . . . . . . . . . . . . . . . . Graham Sutton
Assistant Sound Editor . . . . . . . . . . . . . . . Steve Mayer
Assistant Dialogue Editor . . . . . . . . . . . . . . Robin Quinn
Assistant ADR Editor . . . . . . . . . . . . Foluso Aribigbola
Assistant Foley Editor . . . . . . . . . . . . . . . . Hugo Adams
Assistant Music Editor . . . . . . . . . . . . . . Abigail Doyle

Make-up Artists . . . . . . . . Deborah Jarvis, Sharon Martin,
Kate J. Thompson, Norma Webb
Hairdressers . . . . . . . . . . . Anita Burger, Astrid Schikorra,
Loulia Sheppard

Barber . . . . . . . . . . . . . . . . . . . . . . . . Eric Scruby

Costume Supervisor . . . . . . . . . . . . . . . Clare Spragge
Assistant Costume Designer. . . . . . . . . . . . . . Anna Kot
Wardrobe Assistants. . . . . . Andrew Hunt, Sophie Norinder, Sunita Singh
Additional Wardrobe Assistants . . . Stephen Miles, Jane Petrie

Gaffer . . . . . . . . . . . . . . . . . . . . . . . Pat Grosswendt
Best Boy . . . . . . . . . . . . . . . . . . . . . . . Liam McGill
Electricians . . . . . . . . . . . . . Robert Cuddy, Sam Bloor, Gary Nolan, Martin Welland, Iwan Williams, Neil Munro, Ron Shane
Generator Operator . . . . . . . . . . . . . . . Andrew Purdy

Art Director. . . . . . . . . . . . . . . . . . . . Sarah Hauldren
Property Buyers. . . . . . . . . . . . . . Ray Lee, Fergus Clegg
Assistant Art Director. . . . . . . . . . . . . . . . . Matt Gray
Standby Art Director. . . . . . . . . . . . . . . . James Foster
Draughtsperson . . . . . . . . . . . . . Helen A. Xenopoulos
Art Department Coordinator. . . . . . . . . Shirley Robinson
Researcher. . . . . . . . . . . . . . . . . . . . . Celia Barnett
Art Department Assistant. . . . . . . . . . . . . . Lotta Wolgers

Property Master . . . . . . . . . . . . . . . . . David Balfour
Location Property Master . . . . . . . . . . . . . . John Wells
Property Storeperson . . . . . . . . . . . . . . . Keith Vowles
Chargehand Dresser. . . . . . . . . . . . . . . Lawrence Wells
Dressing Props. . . . . . . . . Marlon Cole, David Cheesman, Mark Geeson, William Wells
Dressing Prop Trainee . . . . . . . . . . . . . . Gary Dawson
Standby Props. . . . . . . . . . . . Robert Hill, Gregor Telfer
Property Department Coordinator . . . . . . Maria Newsham

Construction Manager. . . . . . . . . . . . . Tony Graysmark
Construction Buyer . . . . . . . . . . . . Margaret Graysmark
Construction H.O.D. . . . . . . . . . . . . . . . Chris Brown
Supervising Carpenter. . . . . . . . . . . . . Bryce Johnstone
Carpenters . . . . . . . . John McGoldrick, Hugh McKenzie, Joseph Newman, John Porter, Terence Simpson, Richard Shackleton, Terry Thomson
H.O.D. Scenic . . . . . . . . . . . . . . . . . . Adrian Start
Painters. . . . . . . . . . . . . . Kevin Hopkins, Roy Martin, Douglas Regan, Glenn Start, Matthew Start, John Watts, Michael Weaver
H.O.D. Rigger. . . . . . . . . . . . . . . . . . Ronald Meeks
Rigger . . . . . . . . . . . . . . . . . . . . . Robert Gurney
H.O.D. Stagehand. . . . . . . . . . . . . . . . . . Keith Muir
Stagehands . . . . . . . . . . . . . . . . . . . . Clive Drinkall, Michael Driscoll
H.O.D. Plasterer . . . . . . . . . . . . . . . Allan B. Croucher
Plasterers. . . . . . . . . . . . . . Ian McFadyen, Barry Sams, Keith Shannon

Standby Carpenter . . . . . . . . . . . . . Colin Woodbridge

Standby Painter . . . . . . . . . . . . . . . . . . Albert Roper
Standby Rigger. . . . . . . . . . . . . . . . Raymond Flindall
Standby Stagehand . . . . . . . . . . . . . . . . . James Muir
Standby Plasterer . . . . . . . . . . . . . . . . . . John Mister
Additional Standby Carpenter. . . . . . . . . . . Peter Beasley
Additional Standby Riggers . . . . Darren Flindall, Sid Hinson

Drapes Master . . . . . . . . . . . . . . . . . . . . Colin Fox
Drapes Assistant . . . . . . . . . . . . . . . . . . Frank Howe

Special Effects Supervisor . . . . . . . . . . . . Stuart Brisdon
Special Effects Technician . . . . . . . . . . Mark Haddenham

Home Economist . . . . . . . . . . . . . . . . . Debbie Brodie
Assistant Home Economists . . . Katherine Tidy, Gina Stewart

For Film Council's Premiere Fund

Business Affairs . . . . . . . . Jackie O'Sullivan, Gillian Clyde
Production Finance. . . . . . . . . . . . . . . . . Vince Holden
Production Executives. . . Brock Norman Brock, Luke Morris

Music Produced by . . . . . . . . . . . . . . . Maggie Rodford, Air-Edel Associates Ltd.
Assisted by. . . . . . . . . . . . . . . . . . . . . . Vicky Quinn
Music Orchestrated by . . . . . Patrick Doyle, James Shearman & Lawrence Ashmore
Music Conducted by. . . . . . . . . . . . . . . James Shearman
Music Recorded & Mixed by. . . . . . . . . . . Nick Wollage
Assisted by. . . . . . . . . Ion Metsovitis & Yann McCullough
Music Recorded & Mixed at . . . Air-Edel Recording Studios, London
Musicians Contractor . . . . . . . . . . . . . . . Tonia Davall
Music Preparation. . . . . . . . . . . . . . . . . . Tony Stanton

Featured Musicians

Guitar: . . . . . . . . . . . . John Parricelli & Richard Bolton
1st Violin: . . . . . . . . . . . . . . . Perry Montague-Mason
Bass: . . . . . . . . . . . . . . . . . . . . . . . . . Andy Pask
2nd Violin: . . . . . . . . . Patrick Kiernan & Chris Tombling
Drums: . . . . . . . . . . . . . . . . . . . . . . Ralph Salmins
Viola: . . . . . . . . . . . . . Bruce White, Ivo Van Der Werff
Woodwinds: . . . . . . . . . Jamie Talbot, Nicholas Bucknall
Cello: . . . . . . . . . . . . . . . . . . . . . . . James Potter
Harp: . . . . . . . . . . . . . . . . . . . . . . . . Hugh Webb
Piano: . . . . . . . . . Christopher Northam, Brian Gascoigne
Accordion: . . . . . . . . . . . . . . . . . . . . Eddie Hession

Health & Safety Advisors . . . . . . Jason Curtis, Andy Watson
Unit Nurse. . . . . . . . . . . . . . . . . . . . . . Patricia Barr
Construction Nurse. . . . . . . . . . . . . . . . . . Ruth Nicol
Medical Cover . . . . . . . . . . Capital Medical Services Ltd.

Stunt Coordinator . . . . . . . . . . . . . . . . Dinny Powell
Riding Double. . . . . . . . . . . . . . . . . . . . Abbi Collins
Horse Handler. . . . . . . . . . . . . . . . . . . . . Steve Dent
Pip the Dog . . . . . . . . . . . . . . . . . . . . . . . Widget
Dog Handler. . . . . . . . . . . . Kay Raven, Animals O Kay

Stand-ins . . . . . Joan Field, Gary Messer, David Oliver, Bella Sabbagh

Dialogue Coach . . . . . Julia Wilson-Dixon

Technical Advisors

Butler . . . . . Arthur Inch
Cook . . . . . Ruth Mott
Parlour Maid . . . . . Violet Liddle
Pheasant Shoot . . . . . Ron Puttock
Piano Tutor . . . . . Christopher Northam
Ivor Novello Consultant . . . . . David Slattery-Christy
Bridge Tutor . . . . . Ned Paul
Billiards Tutor . . . . . Kevin Walker

FT2 Trainees . . . . . Alan Harrison, Lisa Inman, Stuart Mackay, Nneka Meka
Work Experience . . . . . Rebecca Farrant, Rowley Samuel

Transport Coordinator . . . . . Roy Clarke
Unit Drivers . . . . . Terry Collins, Clive Crawley, Gerry Floyd, Len Furssedonn, Simon Hudnot, Stanley Surkin, Barry Stevenson

Catering . . . . . Chorley Bunce Meals on a Mission Ltd.
Caterers . . . . . Mark Bunce, Dave Chorley, Phil Churchfield

Facility & Truck Drivers . . . Daniel Brown, George Corrigan, Rob Hanson, Phil Haughton, Bob McGovern, John McMeekin, John Reid, Phil Richman, Dean Roberts, Steve Rose, Gary Sutch, Bob Turner

Security . . . . . Lew Morgan, Tony Cuomo, Terry Green, Scott Reid

Re-Recording Mixer Assistant . . . . . Nigel Bennett
ADR/Foley Mixers . . . . . Ed Colyer, John Bateman
ADR/Foley Mixer Assistants . . . . David Tyler, Esther Smith
Foley Mixer . . . . . Mark Lafbery
ADR Mixer . . . . . Paul Carr
Foley Artists . . . . . Peter Burgis, Andi Derrick, Julie Ankerson, John Fewell

Post-Production Consultancy . . . . . Steve Harrow
Steeple Post-Production Services Ltd.

Legal Services U.S. . . . . . George Sheanshang
Legal Services U.K. . . . . . Barry Smith, Simon Hall
Richards Butler

Insurance Services provided by . . . . AON/Albert G. Ruben
Kevin O'Shea

Camera and Lenses . . . . . Panavision U.K.
Lighting Equipment . . . . . Lee Lighting Ltd.

Editing Equipment . . . . . Orbit Digital LLC
Hyperactive Broadcast Video Hire
Cranes . . . . . Nationwide Access Ltd.
Radios . . . . . Wavevend Radio Communications Ltd.
Color by . . . . . Technicolor Ltd.
Color Grader . . . . . Peter Hunt
Negative Cutting . . . . . Professional Negative Cutting Ltd.
Digital Effects . . . . . Jim Henson's Creature Shop
Film Scanning & Recording Services by Cinesite (Europe) Ltd.
Stuart Pearson, Simon Hughes, Simon Minshall
Titles and Opticals . . . . . Cineimage
Steve Boag, Martin Bullard, Matthew Symonds
Sound Re-Recorded at . . . . . Shepperton Film Studios
Post-Production Facilities . . . . . Shepperton Film Studios
ADR/Foley Studio . . . . . Shepperton Film Studios
Foley Studio . . . . . Twickenham Film Studios Ltd.
Stills Processing . . . . . Visions
Robin Bell
Telecine of Dailies . . . . . Midnight Transfer
Sound Transfer . . . . . Synxspeed Post-Production Ltd.
Post-Production Script . . . . . Sapex Scripts
Armourer . . . . . Perdix Firearms
Charlie Bodycombe
Crowd Casting . . . . . The Casting Collective Ltd.
Costumiers . . . . . Cosprop Ltd.
Wigs supplied by . . . . . The London & New York Wig Co.
Action Vehicles . . . . . Motorhouse Hire Ltd.
John Geary
Special Effects . . . . . United Special Effects Ltd.
Transport Facilities supplied by . . . . . Lays International Ltd.
Movie Makers Facilities
On-Set Location Services Ltd.
Studio Workshops Ltd.
Film 4x4 Ltd.

Location Filming at Syon House by kind permission of . . . . . His Grace The Duke of Northumberland

Banking Finance provided by . . Dexia-Banque Internationale a Luxembourg S.A.

Completion Guaranty provided by . . . . . International Film Guarantors
Luke Randolph

Rushes Theatre Projectionist . . . . . Ray Pascoe
Shipping . . . . . AEI, Danzas Ltd.
World Wide Express
Travel . . . . . CL Travel Consultants
Publicity . . . . . McDonald & Rutter
U.K. Payroll Service . . . . . Axium (U.K.) Ltd.
U.S. Payroll Service . . . . . Axium Entertainment Services
DTS Technical Support Engineer . . . . . Rod Duggan

The Producers Wish to Thank
Sam Cohn
Donna Gigliotti
Stephen Frears
Pam Dixon Mickelson
Elmer Balaban

Chanel Joaillerie, Tessier's Ltd., De Gournay Ltd.

Gary Brady, Maxine Davidson, John Ensby, Avy Eschenasy, Rob Garvey, Hortense Izac, Pat McEnallay, John Mellor, Ian Neil, Nigel Palmer, Anita Patel, Paul Olliver, Nick Pocock, Anita Serwacki, Hugh Whittaker, Thorney Court Management & Staff

Originated on Motion Picture Film from Kodak

Color by Technicolor

Filmed with Panavision Cameras and Lenses supplied by Panavision U.K.

"Waltz of My Heart"
Performed by Christopher Northam
Composed by Ivor Novello & Christopher V. Hassall
©Chappell/Music Limited
By Kind Permission of Warner/Chappell Music Ltd.

"Glamorous Night"
Performed by Christopher Northam
Composed by Ivor Novello & Christopher V. Hassall
© Chappell/Music Limited
By Kind Permission of Warner/Chappell Music Ltd.

"Nuts in May"
Sung by Jeremy Northam
Composed by Ivor Novello & P.G. Wodehouse
© Ascherberg Hopwood & Crew Limited
By Kind Permission of Warner/Chappell Music Ltd.

"The Land of Might-Have-Been"
Sung by Jeremy Northam
Composed by Ivor Novello & Edward Moore
© Ascherberg Hopwood & Crew Limited
By Kind Permission of Warner/Chappell Music Ltd.

"And Her Mother Came Too"
Sung by Jeremy Northam
Composed by Ivor Novello & Dion Titheradge
© Ascherberg Hopwood & Crew Limited
By Kind Permission of
Warner/Chappell Music Ltd.

"I Can Give You the Starlight"
Sung by Jeremy Northam
Composed by Ivor Novello & Christopher V. Hassall
© Chappell/Music Limited
By Kind Permission of Warner/Chappell Music Ltd.

"What a Duke Should Be"
Sung by Jeremy Northam
Composed by Ivor Novello & Clifford Grey
© Ascherberg Hopwood & Crew Limited
By Kind Permission of Warner/Chappell Music Ltd.

"Why Isn't It You"
Sung by Jeremy Northam
Composed by Ivor Novello & Christopher V. Hassall
© Chappell/Music Limited
By Kind Permission of Warner/Chappell Music Ltd.

"Keep the Home Fires Burning"
Performed by Jeremy Northam
Composed by Ivor Novello & Lena Guilbert Ford
© Ascherberg Hopwood & Crew Limited
By Kind Permission of Warner/Chappell Music Ltd.

"The Way It's Meant to Be"
Sung by Abigail Doyle
Music by Patrick Doyle
Lyrics by Robert Altman & Abigail Doyle
© Air-Edel Associates Ltd.
By Kind Permission of Air-Edel Associates Ltd.

Soundtrack Available on Decca Records



Receipts collected and distributed by
National Film Trustee Company Limited

Filmed on location in London & at Shepperton Studios, England

Made with the support of the Film Council Premiere Fund

Film Council Lottery Funded

Worldwide Sales by Capitol Films

MPAA Rating: R (for some language and brief sexuality)

Dolby Quad, in selected theaters

Running Time: 137 minutes Aspect Ratio: 2:35/1 [Scope]

www.gosfordparkmovie.com

A USA Films Release